SIGNS AND WONDERS

INTERNATIONAL THEOLOGICAL COMMENTARY

George A.F. Knight and Fredrick Carlson Holmgren,
General Editors

SIGNS AND WONDERS

A Commentary on the Book of
Daniel

ROBERT A. ANDERSON

WM. B. EERDMANS PUBL. CO., GRAND RAPIDS
THE HANDSEL PRESS LTD, EDINBURGH

For Jean

Copyright © 1984 by Wm. B. Eerdmans Publishing Company

First published 1984 by William B. Eerdmans Publishing Company
255 Jefferson Ave. SE, Grand Rapids, MI 49503
and
The Handsel Press Limited
33 Montgomery Street, Edinburgh EH7 5JX

Eerdmans edition 0-8028-1038-1
Handsel edition 0 905312 30 9

Library of Congress Cataloging in Publication Data

Anderson, Robert A. (Robert Andrew), 1928—
    Signs and wonders.
    (International theological commentary)
    Bibliography: p. 157.
    1. Bible. O.T. Daniel—Commentaries. I. Title.
    II. Series.
BS1555.3.A52   1983   224'.507   83-16602
        ISBN 0-8028-1038-1

Scripture quotations are from the Revised Standard Version of the Bible,
copyrighted 1946, 1952 © 1971, 1973.

CONTENTS

EDITORS' PREFACE

The Old Testament alive in the Church: this is the goal of the *International Theological Commentary*. Arising out of changing, unsettled times, this Scripture speaks with an authentic voice to our own troubled world. It witnesses to God's ongoing purpose and to his caring presence in the universe without ignoring those experiences of life that cause one to question his existence and love. This commentary series is written by front rank scholars who treasure the life of faith.

Addressed to ministers and Christian educators, the *International Theological Commentary* moves beyond the usual critical-historical approach to the Bible and offers a *theological* interpretation of the Hebrew text. The authors of these volumes, therefore, engaging larger textual units of the biblical writings, assist the reader in the appreciation of the theology underlying the text as well as its place in the thought of the Hebrew Scriptures. But more, since the Bible is the book of the believing community, its text in consequence has acquired ever more meaning through an ongoing interpretation. This growth of interpretation may be found both within the Bible itself and in the continuing scholarship of the Church.

Contributors to the *International Theological Commentary* are Christians — persons who affirm the witness of the New Testament concerning Jesus Christ. For Christians, the Bible is *one* scripture containing the Old and New Testaments. For this reason, a commentary on the Old Testament may not ignore the second part of the canon, namely, the New Testament.

Since its beginning, the Church has recognized a special relationship between the two Testaments. But the precise character of this bond has been difficult to define. Thousands of books and articles have discussed the issue. The diversity of views represented in these publications make us aware that the Church is not of one mind in expressing the "how" of this relationship. The authors of this commentary share a developing consensus that any serious explanation of the Old Testament's relationship to the New will uphold the integrity of the Old Testament. Even though Christianity is rooted in the soil of the Hebrew Scriptures, the biblical interpreter must take care lest he "christianize" these Scriptures.

Authors writing in this commentary will, no doubt, hold varied views concerning *how* the Old Testament relates to the New. No attempt has been made to dictate one viewpoint in this matter. With the whole Church, we are convinced that the relationship between the two Testaments is real and substantial. But we recognize also the diversity of opinions among Christian scholars when they attempt to articulate fully the nature of this relationship.

In addition to the Christian Church, there exists another people for whom the Old Testament is important, namely, the Jewish community. Both Jews and Christians claim the Hebrew Bible as Scripture. Jews believe that the basic teachings of this Scripture point toward, and are developed by, the Talmud, which assumed its present form about A.D. 500. Christians, on the other hand, hold that the Old Testament finds its fulfillment in the New Testament. The Hebrew Bible, therefore, "belongs" to both the Church and the Synagogue.

Recent studies have demonstrated how profoundly early Christianity reflects a Jewish character. This fact is not surprising because the Christian movement arose out of the context of first-century Judaism. Further, Jesus himself was Jewish, as were the first Christians. It is to be expected, therefore, that Jewish and Christian interpretations of the Hebrew Bible will reveal similarities *and* disparities. Such is the case. The authors of the *International Theological Commentary* will refer to the various Jewish traditions that they consider important for an appreciation of the Old Testament text. Such references will enrich our understanding of certain biblical passages and, as an extra gift, offer us insight into the relationship of Judaism to early Christianity.

An important second aspect of the present series is its *international* character. In the past, Western church leaders were considered to be *the* leaders of the Church — at least by those living in the West! The theology and biblical exegesis done by these scholars dominated the thinking of the Church. Most commen-

taries were produced in the Western world and reflected the life-
style, needs, and thoughts of its civilization. But the Christian
Church is a worldwide community. People who belong to this
universal Church reflect differing thoughts, needs, and lifestyles.

Today the fastest growing churches in the world are to be
found, not in the West, but in Africa, Indonesia, South America,
Korea, Taiwan, and elsewhere. By the end of this century, Christians in these areas will outnumber those who live in the West.
In our age, especially, a commentary on the Bible must transcend
the parochialism of Western civilization and be sensitive to issues
that are the special problems of persons who live outside of the
"Christian" West, issues such as race relations, personal survival
and fulfillment, liberation, revolution, famine, tyranny, disease,
war, the poor, religion and state. Inspired of God, the authors
of the Old Testament knew what life is like on the edge of existence. They addressed themselves to everyday people who often
faced more than everyday problems. Refusing to limit God to the
"spiritual," they portrayed him as one who heard and knew the
cries of people in pain (see Exod. 3:7-8). The contributors to the
International Theological Commentary are persons who prize the writings of these biblical authors as a word of life to our world today.
They read the Hebrew Scriptures in the twin contexts of ancient
Israel and our modern day.

The scholars selected as contributors underscore the international aspect of the Commentary. Representing very different
geographical, ideological, and ecclesiastical backgrounds, they
come from over seventeen countries. Besides scholars from such
traditional countries as England, Scotland, France, Italy,
Switzerland, Canada, New Zealand, Australia, South Africa, and
the United States, contributors from the following places are included: Israel, Indonesia, India, Thailand, Singapore, Taiwan,
and countries of Eastern Europe. Such diversity makes for rich-
ness of thought. Christian scholars living in Buddhist, Muslim,
or Socialist lands may be able to offer the World Church insights
into the biblical message — insights to which the scholarship of
the West could be blind.

The proclamation of the biblical message is the focal concern
of the *International Theological Commentary*. Generally speaking, the
authors of these commentaries value the historical-critical studies
of past scholars, but they are convinced that these studies by

themselves are not enough. The Bible is more than an object of critical study; it is the revelation of God. In the written Word, God has disclosed himself and his will to humankind. Our authors see themselves as servants of the Word which, when rightly received, brings *shalom* to both the individual and the community.

The book of Daniel is widely regarded as the Bible's first major apocalyptic work. There is a measure of truth in this claim, but it tends to obscure other important features of the book.

This commentary endeavours to place the apocalyptic element within its proper biblical and cultural perspective. However, it also seeks to give due attention to the book of Daniel as a document portraying the pressures exerted on the Judaism of the time, and the response that was made to those pressures — a response of faithfulness and obedience. Like situations may develop at any time in the life of the Church or Synagogue. The book of Daniel may be one of our surest guides and one of our clearest sources of hope.

GEORGE A. F. KNIGHT
FREDRICK CARLSON HOLMGREN

AUTHOR'S PREFACE

The contents of this commentary have necessarily been dictated by the nature of the series for which it has been written. Its indebtedness to a number of recent commentaries on the book of Daniel will, I trust, be obvious, for no attempt has been made to disguise that fact. Indeed, some good purpose will have been achieved if the scholarly work of others has been offered in a form that is more readily appreciated by those for whom this series is designed. There are, of course, many places where this commentary departs from hitherto published positions and where the specific viewpoint of the author is apparent.

This work also attempts to present a more positive attitude towards Judaism and Jewish practices. Though Christian scholars are quickly moving away from the tendency to caricature their sister faith, a good deal of ground is still to be gained. One point where some advance may be made is in the simple departure from the use of B.C. and A.D. and the employment of the more ecumenical B.C.E. (Before the Common Era) and C.E. (Common Era). This may seem of little consequence, but it is a habit worth acquiring, especially when dealing with areas of study where Jewish and Christian scholars are colleagues.

The commentary itself was written while I was enjoying the comfort and the atmosphere of the Oxford Centre for Postgraduate Hebrew Studies as a Visiting Scholar in 1981. I should like to take this opportunity to express my gratitude to the Principal of the Centre, Dr. David Patterson, and to the staff for all their kindness and assistance.

Finally, I dedicate this book to my wife Jean, whose forbearance and patient help have stood me in good stead especially during a decade and a half when I was both an administrator and an academic.

Melbourne   R.A.A.
May 1982

INTRODUCTION

So far as the date of composition of the extant work is concerned, the book of Daniel is generally regarded as the latest of the canonical Hebrew Scriptures. That some, if not all, of the stories found within the first six chapters have a lengthy prehistory is acknowledged, but so compelling is the evidence in favour of placing the final promulgation within the period of the persecution of the Jews under Antiochus IV Epiphanes (175-164 B.C.E.) that it is possible almost to pinpoint, not only the year, but the month when it reached its present form. It is unlikely that any other biblical book is capable of such accurate dating.

It is customary to describe Daniel as an 'apocalyptic' work. Such a designation can be somewhat misleading, for it applies, in the main, only to some of the chapters, i.e., 2 and 7 – 12. Even in the latter grouping a considerable amount of material is of a nonapocalyptic character, and the type of apocalyptic that does appear is not of an advanced kind. In reading the book of Daniel it is wise not to allow general descriptions of apocalyptic to obtrude themselves, and also to bear in mind that the author(s) uses a variety of literary forms and has been subject not to one influence, but to many. It is not as absurd as it may at first appear to suggest that the author of Daniel had access to all the books that came to make up the canon of the Hebrew Scriptures.

Scholarly discussion in recent years has shown how marked are the links between prophecy and apocalyptic, and what applies in a general way may also hold for an individual book such as Daniel where apocalyptic features are in fact present. But what is of significance in approaching Daniel is not so much how these general influences have shaped the work, but how the author used specific prophetic texts, i.e., how he consciously bound his words, and the community for which he wrote, to the great tradition of the prophets. One example of this is his declaration in the opening verses of the book that it was God who gave the king of Judah into the hands of the Babylonian monarch Nebuchad-nezzar. In this interpretation he is in the goodly company of Jeremiah, Ezekiel, and Deutero-Isaiah.

Another example, and one which necessarily receives lengthy treatment in the commentary, is the interpretation he placed on Jer. 25:12 and 29:10 in considering the duration of the Exile. The author was at pains to point out that what he declared to his contemporaries had on it the imprimatur of the great prophet of the Exile, Jeremiah. A further example of the recollection and re-presentation of the prophetic word is to be found in Dan. 11:33 and 12:3 in particular, where there is something akin to a mid-rash or commentary on the so-called Fourth Servant Song of Isa. 52:13 – 53:12. The importance of the author's use of these verses goes far beyond the presence here of a mere passing commentary on an earlier text. Nor is it limited to the fact that this is one further instance of the close relationship that exists between prophecy and apocalyptic. At stake is not merely the legitimacy of descent of the latter but the legitimate descent of the com-munity of which the author is a member. It is this community, so he argues, that is the bearer of the prophetic word. This is no inconsequential assertion and certainly not one that may be dis-missed out of hand simply because of any later claim to such a role.

It can also be shown that Daniel's links with tradition extend beyond the use of prophetic texts. The prayer in 2:20-23 exhibits clear dependence on a number of texts in the Writings (the third section of the Hebrew canon), e.g., Pss. 41:14; 106:48; 113:2; Job 12:12, 13; Neh. 9:5; and Esth. 1:13. A similar influence may be discerned in the prayer of 9:4-19, which gives clear indications of dependence on such texts as Neh. 1:5, 6, 11; 9:2, 8, 17, as well as Ezra 9:15.

Much has been written in recent times of the distinct parallels between the court-motif of the Joseph story and that of the early chapters of Daniel. Attention must also be given to what the book says of the hero, Daniel himself. What emerges even from a cur-sory examination is that Daniel is not only a visionary and a person of considerable accomplishments, but above all a man of Torah.

Though attempts to find a possible connection between the

Daniel of the book and some legendary wise man bearing the same or a similar name have unearthed some interesting information, they have proved to be less than conclusive so far as their chief aim was concerned. It would now appear best to allow Daniel to stand in his own right. The name Daniel may well have been chosen for the message it conveys, 'God judges' or 'God has judged'. The hero of the book appears as the exemplar of faithfulness. He is a gifted young man of outstanding natural qualities, a youth 'without blemish, handsome and skilful in all wisdom, endowed with knowledge, understanding learning . . .' (1:4). Important as these attributes are, what the author extols above all else is the young man's loyalty to the precepts of his faith. It was this persistent and unflinching fidelity that earned him the special favour of God. The young Daniel is seen as the epitome of the faithful Jew, surrounded by all the enticements of an alien culture, yet standing stalwart against all these, refusing to compromise either belief or practice. The natural outcome of such unswerving obedience was increased wisdom and knowledge, qualities that were to be amply demonstrated in certain of the stories related of him.

If Daniel exemplified faithfulness, he no less personified the man of prayer. This is certainly the central feature of ch. 6 and the precondition of divine inspiration in ch. 9.

What we have in the book of Daniel is a life of faithfulness, obedience, and prayer. This is presented in an engaging and popularising manner, and serves as both exhortation and inspiration to those who might find themselves in parallel circumstances. Daniel's great strength and the firmness of his resolve arose from this adherence to Torah. As such, he stood in a long line of succession stretching back as far as Moses and embracing such mentors as Amos, Isaiah, and Ezra.

This recognition of the Torah-based character of Daniel, together with the book's use of and links with a wide range of other canonical literature, suggests an ecumenicity of outlook and spirit perhaps without parallel in the OT, and may well reinforce not only the view that the date of final composition is late, but that the author had ready access to the remainder of the canon. It was these qualities and perspectives that must have led to the book's receiving a large measure of acceptance. It is not difficult to imagine that such a work had immediate popular appeal, and unless the latter is excluded as a factor in the process which led to eventual canonisation good reasons can be discerned why this status was attained. It may well be argued that, to all intents and purposes, the book of Daniel was 'canonised' (though the use of this word is not without objection) shortly after the time of its completion. The popularly held view that it was not until the closing decades of the first century C.E., at the so-called Council of Jamnia (Javneh), that official endorsement was given the books of the Hebrew canon, and in particular those of its third section, the Writings, has been under serious scholarly attack of late, and it may well be that this aspect at least of the history of canonisation will have to be drastically revised. In any case, Jamnia or not, the acceptance in fact and in practice of each book is quite another matter.

The place of Daniel in the canon and its relationship to other works which were afforded similar status are important questions. Also of importance, however, is the matter of the book's relationship to those writings which did not receive such recognition. Of these the most noteworthy is 1 Maccabees, for this work in particular gives the background to many of the events that are related or alluded to in Daniel 7 – 12 (see especially 1 Macc. 1 – 5). Of lesser significance, though useful reading, is 2 Maccabees, particularly chs. 1 – 6, material which sometimes supplements the 1 Maccabees account. It is worth noting that its rather embellished treatment is historically less reliable than that of 1 Maccabees. Other works which are either apocryphal or pseudepigraphal and which have a bearing on the Daniel material include the book of Jubilees, which may be dated somewhere between 160 and 140 B.C.E., the Testament (or Assumption) of Moses, parts of which probably come from the time of Antiochus IV Epiphanes, and 1 Enoch (or Ethiopic Enoch). One section of the last mentioned, chs. 83 – 90, dates from the period 164-160 B.C.E. Another, chs. 1 – 36, most likely originated prior to 175 B.C.E., while it is possible that chs. 72 – 82 are from the 3rd cent. B.C.E. All of these books or sections of books throw light on the development of Hebrew religious literature during the period from which Daniel emanates. This is also true of much of the material that has been discovered in recent decades in the vicinity of the Dead Sea. Some knowledge of these nonbiblical Jewish writings will appreciably enhance the mod-ern-day reader's understanding of the book of Daniel.

Because of its position at the end of the OT, so to speak, and within or at the beginning of the intertestamental period, the book of Daniel has special significance for the study of the NT. If E. Käsemann is correct in his assertion that 'apocalyptic is the mother of Christian theology' (*NT Questions of Today*, 137), this book, even when the extent of its apocalyptic nature has been accurately assessed, must be seen to have added significance. This lies not in any direct or immediate links that may be thought to exist between certain concepts and statements in Daniel and their supposed fulfilment in the NT, but rather in the stream of influence in which Daniel itself was caught up, and which flowed on down to the earliest days of the Church.

CHAPTER 1

TORAH AND OBEDIENCE
Daniel 1:1-21

1-2 The book of Daniel opens on a markedly despondent note. The city of Jerusalem has been besieged by the army of Nebuchadnezzar, king of Babylon, and, by implication, it has fallen into his hands. But the most striking observation is that this catastrophe has occurred not merely because of the strength of arms of a foreign monarch but by the very action of God himself (v. 2).

Reference is often made to a historical inaccuracy within these opening verses. This matter is treated at length in the major commentaries, and the inquiring reader is directed to these. All that needs to be said here is that in all probability the author of Daniel was influenced by the statements in 2 Chr. 36:5-7 and 2 Kgs. 24:1. One further point that should be noted at the outset is that historical inexactitudes are not infrequent in this book. Though matters of this nature may not be passed over lightly, we should guard ourselves against allowing them to become so obtrusive that they hide the real issues.

What is of more immediate importance in the brief historical superscription is not the name of the Judean king, nor the stated date of the siege, but the judgment that Jerusalem fell because it was the will of the God of Israel that such a fate should befall the Holy City. This is stated clearly and emphatically: 'The LORD gave Jehoiakim . . . into his hand . . .' (v. 2a).

The author of Daniel is not alone in this judgment. He is in the company of the prophet Jeremiah who proclaimed that just such an event would occur, and that it was no less than divine punishment for the sins of the nation's leaders (e.g., Jer. 21:1-7 and 25:8-14). Neither the promise of eventual return to their own land (Jer. 50:19) nor the prediction of the eventual overthrow of

Babylon (Jer. 25:12-15 and 50:1-16) could relieve the pain of divine chastisement inflicted by an alien power bent on the pillage and destruction of the innocent along with the guilty. The exilic prophet Ezekiel had interpreted the calamitous events of his day in a similar vein (Ezek. 2:1ff.; 4:1ff.; 6:1ff.). Moreover, the book of Lamentations was a further reminder that the destruction of Jerusalem and the deportation of many of its inhabitants were not the casual outcome of political and military struggle but the decree of the nation's God.

The inexact dating in v. 1 does pose a problem for the meticulous historian. The assertion of direct and cataclysmic intervention on the part of God, however, is no less a problem for the theologian or, for that matter, for anyone who is prepared to attempt to understand ancient Israel's relationship to God in other than the most simple mechanistic terms. How is one to understand God's dealings with his covenant people and, seemingly, the use of foreign nations to inculcate the lesson of obedience? It is far easier to raise the question than it is to supply an adequate answer. Yet, if we are to maintain integrity in our interpretation of the ancient biblical record, we must attempt an answer. It does justice neither to the material before us, nor to the inquiring mind that seeks to grapple with that material as the Word of God, simply to gloss over such an issue.

What we can say with some confidence, on the basis of the prophetic preaching from Amos to Ezekiel, is that there was in OT times the conviction that disobedience to the divine will carries with it the seeds of destruction. The great prophets laid the blame for this disobedience, in the main, at the feet of the leaders, both temporal and spiritual. Kings and princes, priests and false prophets, are singled out for particular mention. Yet they are only part of the nation. The process of disobedience and the subsequent process of destruction catch up the whole people, innocent and guilty alike, the leaders and the led, for they are all bound in the same bundle of life. Not only the wayward shepherds suffer but the sheep also.

From another perspective, it can readily be seen that no small nation, obedient or disobedient, could have withstood the onslaught of Nebuchadnezzar's armies. This point alone contrives further to compound the theological difficulties. Several pertinent questions present themselves. Would an obedient Judah really have thwarted the expansionist policies of Babylon? Are God's plans for his people subject to the vagaries of human behaviour and the inconsistent consequences of the historical process? Or is it that nations and individuals are shuffled by the deity around some gigantic cosmic chessboard? We learn from the early chapters of the book of Genesis that mankind has freedom to obey or to disobey. What is said of people as such must necessarily be said also of the nations they comprise, Judah or Israel or, for that matter, Babylonia. Any answer to the vexing question of God's dealings with the nations in pursuit of his purpose for Israel and, through it, for the world must take account of this freedom. The answer that does not do so would commit us to the espousal of a fatalistic determinism. But equally unacceptable would be a solution that denied freedom to God.

The opening verses do no more than set the mood and prepare the scene. The extensive accounts in 2 Kgs. 24:1 – 25:20; 2 Chr. 36:5-21; and Jer. 39:1ff. and 52:1-34 provide the details. In the year 586 B.C.E. Jerusalem fell, the walls of the Holy City were demolished, and the temple destroyed. The ark of the covenant, for centuries the most sacred cultic object, disappeared for all time and thousands of Judeans joined their already exiled compatriots in Babylonia. If the political status of the Judeans was desperate, their religious situation was more so. The exiles were bereft of almost all the external supports of faith. The building of a temple on foreign soil was proscribed by Torah, making the offering of sacrifices no longer possible. The great annual pilgrimages could no longer be held. But worse than this, the victory of Marduk, god of the Babylonians, was seemingly the defeat of Yahweh, God of the Judeans. From every outward appearance the God of Israel had fared no better than his people. Were not some of the holy objects of his temple now deposited in the treasure house of Nebuchadnezzar's god?

This, then, is the historical and religious setting of the book of Daniel — or, rather, of the first six chapters. These relate the stories of the man Daniel, his three companions, and various Babylonian monarchs. A closer examination of this material shows that the individual chapters did not come from any one particular period and are, in the main, difficult to date. They did not arise, however, in the period of the sixth-century Exile. The reader of the book of Daniel has to be aware of three time sequences: the

3

ostensible dating of the book (6th cent. B.C.E.), the origin and development of the individual segments of the book (from the 4th to the 2nd cents. B.C.E.), and the date of the final collation, editing, and promulgation (164 B.C.E.).

Daniel, the hero of both the stories and the visions, is presented as having lived throughout the Exile. We are told nothing of his antecedents. There is not the faintest trace of a genealogy. But that point alone is not sufficient to deny him historicity. There may well have been an exile named Daniel in whom the qualities of courage, wisdom, and devotion were remarkably exemplified. If so, he shared this name, or close approximations of it, with great worthies of the past (Ezek. 14:14, 20; 28:3; and the Ugaritic Tale of Aqhat).

3-4 Daniel is introduced as one of several young Israelites of royal blood who have been chosen to take their places in the royal palace in order to serve the Babylonian king (v. 3). The criteria for their selection are interesting. They were to be flawless and handsome young men, skilled in matters of wisdom, with the capacity both to learn and to serve (v. 4). An early rabbinic tradition based on Isa. 39:7 presented Daniel and his companions as eunuchs. This might receive some support from the RSV translation of *sarisim* as 'eunuchs' (v. 3) rather than the preferred 'palace servants', but there is no evidence to suggest that those put under the care of Ashpenaz necessarily were of the same ilk. Moreover, the statement in v. 4 that the youths were 'without blemish', i.e., that they had no bodily defects, seems to put the matter beyond doubt.

5-7 As young men selected for special service the four young Jews were given special privileges during the period of preparation. Not the least of these was the quality of their food and drink: they were to receive a daily allotment from the king's own larder (v. 5).

The first specific reference to Daniel comes in v. 6 where he is mentioned, along with his three companions, first by their Hebrew names and then by names either received from Ashpenaz, the chief of the palace servants (v. 7), or by adoption. A change of name within the OT usually has special significance. It may suggest a certain relationship, a personal characteristic, or sometimes a stipulated function. It is doubtful, however, whether any of these purposes is involved in these stories. In the case of the three companions there is no consistent use of either set of names, Hebrew or Babylonian. The name Daniel is used exclusively throughout the second section of the book (chs. 7 – 12) and is clearly the preferred editorial description in most of the rest of the book. The central hero is addressed as Belteshazzar only by King Nebuchadnezzar (4:6, 15, 16), replies as such once (4:16), and in several other places is referred to as 'Daniel whose name was Belteshazzar' or its equivalent (2:26, 4:8, and 5:12, where the change of name is attributed to Nebuchadnezzar). Any attempt to unravel what might be an early or a late story solely on the basis of change of name is not likely to meet with success.

It was not uncommon for Hebrew heroes to be depicted as serving foreign monarchs. The best-known example of this is Joseph (Gen. 41:37 – 48:22), whose experiences in the court of the pharaoh may well have prompted many features of these stories. Nehemiah is another example (Neh. 1:11 – 2:8), and presumably Ezra was also a functionary of the court (Ezra 7:1-26; see especially v. 14). With notable precedents such as these it would have been strange had there been any voicing of disapproval or even any note of criticism from the author or editor of the book. The decades and centuries of exile and foreign domination had accustomed the Jewish people to coming to terms with the political and social orders imposed on them. No doubt the belief that fundamentally the world was God's creation, and consequently something to be participated in rather than avoided, helped them in this accommodation to circumstances beyond their control. To withdraw from the world is contrary to Jewish tradition. The ghetto was not withdrawal but expulsion. Preservation of the faith and the maintenance of one's own integrity, however, are possible only when the limits of conformity and assimilation are clearly drawn. For the young Daniel, to be chosen to serve the king was an honour. It was an appreciation of his character and his talents, and the means whereby he might serve his God more fully. Yet dangers were evident. As the ensuing stories indicate, there were some practices which he must observe with all his might but others that he must avoid with equal force.

8-16 The pivotal verse of ch. 1 is the eighth. Daniel's decision to abstain from the proffered delicacies was both the touchstone of his religious commitment and the key to his extraordinary advancement. Of course it does not necessarily follow that obedience to the divine command is attended by success, any more than the converse is true. The book of Job makes that point quite explicitly, as does the questioning of Jeremiah (Jer. 12:1) and of Habakkuk (Hab. 1:13). But the book of Daniel was not written as a thesis on theodicy. It was written, rather, to instruct and to inspire those who were forced to live in the midst of hostility, in an environment studded with constant reminders of their subservient position. Though we may rightly speak of Daniel's advancement and success, it has to be recalled that the personal danger he endured was both real and frightening. In this way the author uses the figure of Daniel to speak to his community. The lesson for those who aspired to faithfulness was that obedience to Torah may have concomitant dangers; indeed, it would have. The stories of Daniel are not intended to canvass every possibility; they are stories and not theological treatises. But the message they contain is straightforward and direct, with the aim, not of titillating the intellect, but of confirming the faith of ordinary people. These were men and women beset by the disadvantages of their political and social milieu and encompassed on all sides by the enticement of apostasy.

Seen in this light the young Daniel's resolute decision takes on a new dimension. It is not the mark of an arrogant exclusivism but the outward sign of a determined loyalty. Abstention from certain foods and the observance of certain esoteric practices have undoubted importance in themselves. But what they point to, what they symbolize, is of far greater significance. A reminder of this may preserve us from hasty judgment of the practices of others.

What follows Daniel's decision is no more the placing of the divine imprimatur on asceticism, religious or otherwise, than it is the biblical underwriting of vegetarianism. Both must seek their warrant elsewhere. The scant diet of Daniel and his three friends serves one purpose and only one, and that is to bring into even sharper relief the interior action of God in their preparation. Because of this divine intervention Ashpenaz was spared embarrassment, perhaps even worse (v. 10), and the four young Jews were assured that their God was with them. In refusing what would appear to have been more nourishing food Daniel demonstrated that he was prepared to take the risk that God would undergird his efforts. If the ten days' test proved satisfactory there could be little doubt that, given the strength of their cause and the power of their divine guarantor, they would all handsomely survive. The ten days would soon become three years. The story proceeds to show that in appearance and health they surpassed their fellows (v. 15). But it goes on to say that when later put to the test by Nebuchadnezzar they outstripped all others in wisdom and knowledge (v. 19). Indeed, in these matters their prowess far exceeded that of the Babylonian magicians and enchanters (v. 20).

17-21 The story so far has stressed the imperative of obedience to the divine Torah. A new element is now introduced, the attaining of wisdom. That this was an essential ingredient of the courtier's makeup is first mentioned in v. 4, but in vv. 17 and 20 it begins to take on an importance of its own. The presence of such terms as 'wisdom' and 'understanding' might suggest support for the view that OT apocalyptic is a child of the so-called wisdom movement. But a comparison of the contents of Proverbs, Ecclesiastes, and Job with what is to be found in the book of Daniel points up some clear differences. The wisdom literature of the Hebrew Scriptures is of two main kinds, didactic and reflective. In the former, in the book of Proverbs for example, it was the task of the sage to instruct young men how to comport themselves, how to avoid trouble, and how to lead successful and respectable lives. The clientele were drawn from the upper reaches of society. In the latter, the reflective literature, the traditional wise man cogitated on one or another of the major problems of life as in the book of Job or Ecclesiastes (Qohelet). The wisdom of Daniel is quite other than these two disciplines. It is the product neither of sombre teaching nor of sober reflection. And it has as its subject matter, not advice and discussion, but the weighty matters of the overthrow of kingdoms, of an end of the established order, of judgment and resurrection. What is more, Daniel, the archetype of the apocalyptic wise man, receives this gift by special divine endowment. His discernment is the result of direct divine revelation. There may be traces of the influence of the wisdom movement but these are minimal.

Not only did God give Daniel and his companions 'learning and skill in all letters and wisdom', but Daniel himself 'had understanding in all visions and dreams' (v. 17). It is this unusual and divinely induced perception that figures so largely in the first section of the book. He is able to reveal both the dream and the interpretation to Nebuchadnezzar in ch. 2. In ch. 4 he comes to the help of the king in a similar situation, and in ch. 5 Daniel alone can read the writing on the wall. If Daniel is to be listed among the wise men of the Hebrew Scriptures, he must also appear in the catalogue of seers.

As hero of the book that bears his name, and as representative of the faith and God of Israel, Daniel is pitted against the best that the Babylonian court can muster. This serves both a polemic and an apologetic purpose. The hero may be Daniel, but the power that enables him to rise victoriously over his opponents is the power of the God of Israel. Conversely, the vanquished are not so much the 'Chaldeans' as the gods these magicians and astrologers represent. Thus the tables are turned. Outwardly victory has gone to the gods of the Babylonians (the Exile is the sure sign of that), but the initiated know that in reality this is not so. The God who handed over Jehoiakim to Nebuchadnezzar is the same God who demonstrates his power and makes known his will through his servant Daniel.

As though to underline the strength of the book's central figure we are informed in the closing verse of this chapter that Daniel 'continued until the first year of King Cyrus.' He lived to see the fall of Babylon. This would suggest a lengthy though not impossibly long career. We miss the whole purpose of the book, however, if we engage in arithmetical niceties.

CHAPTER 2

THE INDESTRUCTIBLE KINGDOM
Daniel 2:1-49

The greater part of the first section of the book of Daniel consists of a cycle of Daniel stories of which ch. 2 is the first. This division into two segments of six chapters each has much to commend it. Though the segments share certain common features, and these must not be lost sight of, there are adequate grounds for maintaining the distinction. In a general way chs. 1 – 6 are stories whereas chs. 7 – 12 have to do with a series of visions and their interpretation. In a more detailed examination of the matter the following points emerge:

(i) the Daniel of chs. 1 – 6 is spoken of in the third person whereas, with the exception of the introductory verse of ch. 7, he appears in the first person throughout the second section;

(ii) the divine messages in chs. 1 – 6 are received through the dreams and visionary experiences of foreign monarchs with Daniel acting as interpreter. In chs. 7 – 12, however, Daniel himself has the visions. The interpreters are angelic beings. Daniel's vision in 2:19 is a minor exception to this general description;

(iii) in part of chs. 1 – 6, i.e., ch. 1, ch. 2:13, 17, and 49, and ch. 3, Daniel is accompanied by three compatriots, Hananiah, Mishael, and Azariah. These three have no part whatsoever in chs. 7 – 12.

This fortuitous and useful division of the book should not be allowed to obscure the fact that the first section in particular is far from homogeneous and, what is more, is not entirely unre-

9

lated to the second. Chapter 2, e.g., has more in common with ch. 7 than with any one chapter of the first half of the book. It is far removed from the popular miracle stories of chs. 3 and 6.

Scholarly opinion varies sharply as to the dating of ch. 2. A number of scholars, among them Ginsberg and Hartman, argue for a late 4th-century or early 3rd-cent. B.C.E. date for at least the basic content of the chapter. This basic content or, as Hartman prefers to designate it, 'the primary story', has built on earlier material either in written or oral form. Into the extant written form, which is itself probably a collation of two variant accounts, later additions, namely, vv. 29-30 and 40-43, have been inserted.

Against this is the view of M. Hengel that the content and the intention of ch. 2, and also ch. 7, are so much a part of the finished product's 'theology of history' that it should not be assumed that material of this type constituted 'an independent entity before the origin of the work and was simply taken over by the author' (*Judaism and Hellenism: Studies in Their Encounter in Palestine during the Early Hellenistic Period,* 1:182). As though to compound the difficulties, one of the verses in ch. 2, namely v. 43, which is accepted by Hartman as a late insertion, is employed by Hengel to give force to his argument that the form of the extant material comes from the author of the book. Without further expansion on the point, however, Hengel does state elsewhere in his work that the author had at his disposal 'an old narrative collection of "court stories" . . . which probably included the framework of chapter 2 and chapters 4-6' (*Judaism and Hellenism,* 2:123). This latter statement may soften somewhat the points at issue between Hartman and Hengel, but a clear difference of opinion remains. The tentativeness of some of the scholarly claims should not be seen as detracting from their value.

This brief reference to conflicting scholarly opinion raises another important issue. In many parts of the Bible, not least in the Pentateuch, it is difficult to differentiate between what is primary and what is secondary so far as the extant composition is concerned. The matter is made even more complex when it is remembered that some material circulated in oral form long before it was written down. Furthermore, the whole or part may have been subjected to interpretation, reinterpretation, and modification over the course of centuries. The question arises as to whether we should endeavour to trace the history of the text or whether we should simply allow ourselves to be influenced by the text as it stands and accept the traditionally transmitted view of the provenance and dating of that text. There is such latitude for differing opinions and for disagreements in this area that the least we should do is suspend dogmatic assertions and recognize that our knowledge is far from complete.

What is true of the Bible generally is no less true of each of its constituent parts, even of that complex collection of verses, Daniel 2. Two points emerge from a reading of this chapter. First, it contains a clear demonstration of the prowess of Daniel over the Babylonian magicians and sorcerers and consequently of the superiority of Daniel's God over the local gods. So compelling is this that the king himself is portrayed as acknowledging the One who is 'God of gods and Lord of kings' (v. 47a). It is this victory of the faithful Daniel and his God that would appeal to and give comfort to his compatriots who, while not facing such a rigorous test, would nevertheless find themselves in situations of severe temptation and trial. To this extent there is something of the popular miracle story in ch. 2, but this characteristic is not as sustained here as in chs. 3 and 6. So far as its theme is concerned, this kind of story could have arisen at any time during the exilic or postexilic periods.

The second point emerges from what is said of the four kingdoms and their ultimate displacement by a kingdom established by 'the God of heaven'. This image of successive kingdoms is to be found elsewhere in the book (chs. 7 and 8) and touches on what might be called a 'theology of history'. While it is possible that the raw material of this chapter had currency before the time of the author of the book, in its present form it is so much a part of his theological outlook that it is difficult to delineate what is inherited and what is original. What has come down to him has been thoroughly reworked and made to suit his particular purpose.

1-12 This is the first of Nebuchadnezzar's two dreams; the second forms the substance of ch. 4. The chronological note in v. 1 is not capable of reconciliation with the historical superscription to the book as a whole, nor with the three-year period of Daniel's preparation for court service. There may have been some good reason for adopting that particular date, but whatever it is, it has been lost to us, and no good purpose is served by attempting any kind of correlation. In the end, every such effort is unverifiable conjecture. Much the same type of difficulty is found again and again in the book of Daniel, which shares with much other biblical material a frustrating disregard for chronological exactitude.

Dreams, and the ability to interpret them, played an important role in the ancient world, not least among the Hebrews. It was in a dream that the fleeing patriarch Jacob received the needed assurance of the divine presence and the promise of the land (Gen. 28:12-17). Through his interpretation of the pharaoh's disturbing dreams another exile, Joseph, rose to a position of power and eminence in the land of Egypt (Gen. 41:39-44), providing a literary pattern for the later Daniel. Shortly after his accession to the throne of David his father, Solomon received from God, in a dream, the gift of 'a wise and discerning mind' (1 Kgs. 3:5-14). The list of such experiences is long and impressive, and it was not doubted at the time, nor in later tradition, that this was a very real means of divine communication. Patriarchs and kings, prophets and sages, all could witness to that. In the book of Daniel the hero is both dreamer and interpreter, combining in his person not a little of some of the great figures of the past, Joseph in particular.

Verse 1 closes with the interesting statement that after he had dreamt, Nebuchadnezzar's 'spirit was troubled, and his sleep left him'. Though the sense is quite clear, the question as to whether the king remembered his dream or not fails to be answered by these words alone. Are we to understand that he was denied further sleep by the not uncommon frustration resulting from inability to recall the substance of the dream? Or are we presented here the picture of a man who knew full well what he had dreamt but who was so overcome by it that he lay awake waiting anxiously for break of day? The story seems to require our acceptance of the latter possibility. If this understanding of the story is correct, it is possible to see why the king subjected his magicians and sorcerers to the most rigid of all tests, not merely the interpretation of a dream, but the recounting of the dream itself. Nebuchadnezzar was in a position to ascertain beyond all doubt whether his retainers had the required capacity to render an interpretation other than one concocted simply in order to placate an unstable master. This was the one sure test that he could apply, for he alone knew the content of the dream. He was in the happy position of possessing a firm measure both of their ability and their integrity. For this reason he is presented in the story as becoming increasingly impatient with their temporising. Daniel is given a similar test (v. 26), but it is not accompanied by hectoring or by implied disbelief. No doubt this is to bear out what has been stated in 1:19-20, an appraisal of the hero shared only by the author and his readers.

The appearance in v. 4 of the MT of the words 'in Aramaic' (see RSV footnote), probably a scribal gloss, raises the perplexing question of the bilingualism of the book of Daniel. The MT from 2:4 to the end of ch. 7 is written in Aramaic. This language was widely used throughout the ancient Near East from the 7th cent. B.C.E. and, apart from Daniel, is to be found in two sections of Ezra (4:8 – 6:18 and 7:12-26), as well as in Jer. 10:11 and Gen. 31:47 (two words only). The perplexity arises not from the fact of its use throughout Dan. 2:4 – 7:28 but from the unexpected reversion to Hebrew in 8:1.

There is considerable strength in the argument, advanced in more recent times by R. H. Charles, H. L. Ginsberg, and F. Zimmermann, and adopted by Hartman and Lacocque, among others, that the original language of the whole book was Aramaic. There are points especially within chs. 8 – 12 where a reconstruction of the Hebrew text on the basis of a supposed original Aramaic is helpful to translation. But two clear questions remain. First, why was it thought necessary to translate the opening (1:1 – 2:4a) and closing sections into Hebrew? Second, why was the change to Hebrew made at 8:1? The least satisfactory answer to the first question, but one popularly advanced, is that it was in order that the book should be received into the canon, i.e., an otherwise contraband article was smuggled into the canon by an innocent beginning and ending. A more likely reason is that a work which was to circulate among Hebrew people, particularly those under some duress from foreign authorities, should demonstrably be seen to be part of their own religious and national tradition. A reason advanced in reply to the second question is that the kinship of chs. 2 and 7 would require that they appear in the same tongue. This argument is less than convincing, for it could apply equally to ch. 8. It may be that the choice of the point where once again the national and religious language should be employed was made on solely arbitrary grounds. There is some comfort in being able to agree with Porteous that the linguistic change at the beginning of ch. 8 'seems to have no obvious bearing on the problems of interpretation' (*Daniel*, 40).

As v. 5 indicates, the request of the Chaldeans to be apprised of the content of the dream is sternly rebuffed by Nebuchadnezzar. Either they accept his terms and comply with his demands or they will be dismembered and their houses reduced to ruin. Success, however, will be attended by high honour and great reward. So, by this means, the author both heightens the suspense and prepares the reader for the inevitable outcome (v. 48). The repeated entreaties of the Chaldeans are in vain and serve only to convince the king that they are indeed playing for time. It is the measure of their despair that what is wrung from them is the admission that the request made of them is beyond human capacity to fulfil. It is possible, so they aver, only by means of divine revelation (v. 11). What for the Chaldeans is an excuse is for the author a confession. Not only is the king's dream hidden from human comprehension; so, too, are the events of history.

Verse 12 is a succinct reminder of the ruthlessness of the ancient oriental despot, something that might alarm the modern reader were he not inured to the cruel barbarity of our own time.

13-23 The secondary nature of these verses is attested in that they may be omitted without causing any interruption to the story proper. Verse 24 follows quite smoothly from v. 12. The suggested omission of the words 'went in' in v. 16 (following the text of Theodotion and the Syriac) does not obviate the difficulty. What is said is still very much anticipatory of v. 25. The point, however, is a relatively minor one. In the extant form of ch. 2 (and that after all is the only text before us), these verses have their own important function and the author was seemingly quite undismayed by the repetitive nature of some of his material.

In this chapter Daniel appears on the scene for the first time in v. 13. The young exiled Jew had been prepared for this hour. Schooled in the court of Nebuchadnezzar but nurtured by the Torah and strengthened by the God of his fathers, he is about to be put to the test. It is now to be seen whether what was claimed for him, that he 'had understanding in all visions and dreams'

and that his gifts far outshone those of his Babylonian counter-
parts, had substance or not (1:17-20). Very prudently Daniel
sought out Arioch the chief executioner and the one who must
necessarily carry out the king's decree, and asked of him the
reason for its severity. We are to understand that Arioch now
makes the whole matter known to Daniel, whereupon the latter
receives not only the audience of the king but a stay of execution
permitting him an opportunity to demonstrate his own superior
interpretative talent. But there is more to it than that. Daniel is
by no means carried away by his own reputation. Instead of
acting immediately, he returns to his three companions (v. 17),
who at this crucial point in the story bear their Hebrew names,
Hananiah, Mishael, and Azariah, for they, too, have a task to
perform. Though they appear in this chapter only fleetingly, the
young compatriots are given the important task of interceding
with God (v. 18). In the book of Daniel prayer is regarded with
high seriousness. It is the bulwark against every assault of the
enemy (see ch. 6). Twice in consecutive verses (18 and 19) we
find the expression 'the God of heaven', a divine appellation that
does not appear in preexilic literature, with the sole exception of
Gen. 24:7, but which becomes increasingly common in texts both
biblical and extrabiblical from the postexilic period (e.g., Neh.
1:4; 2:5, 20; Ezra 1:2; 5:11, 12; Jonah 1:9; Jdt. 5:8; cf. 'Lord of
heaven' in Tob. 10:12 and 1 Enoch 13:4). The later abandonment
of this epithet was due most likely to its closeness to the Hellenistic 'Zeus Ouranios'.

   Though early Jewish apocalyptic stands in the line of succession of Hebrew prophecy and shows clear signs of other indige-
nous influences, it also has much in common with its non-Jewish
environment. This is suggested by the use of the word 'mystery'
(*raz, razah*, v. 19), found only in Daniel so far as biblical literature
is concerned, but of Persian origin and strongly suggestive of a
Hellenistic milieu. The climate of Daniel and also of the Qumran
literature is one where the mysteries of God are revealed only to
the select few. One of these is the man Daniel: 'Then the mystery
was revealed to Daniel in a vision of the night' (v. 19). There, in
that brief statement, is contained one of the essential elements of
the book. The God of heaven rules the course of history and
reveals this to his faithful servant.

   At this point the reader is made to await the continuation of the story proper while precedence is given to a Psalm of Thanks-giving (vv. 20-23). This psalm, like those of the Bible generally, should not be passed over hurriedly, for it is in the psalms that we come closest to the religious expression and the theological thought of the ancient Hebrews.

The benediction in the first part of v. 20 is the Aramaic equiv-alent of Pss. 41:14; 106:48; and 113:2; it is a familiar scriptural and later Jewish liturgical invocation. To this everlasting God wisdom and might belong, and the poem proceeds to enumerate the ways in which God both dispenses his wisdom and exercises his power. In his might 'he changes times and seasons' (v. 21), and with this confession of divine omnipotence we are invited to compare the furious but limited power of the one who peremp-torily sought 'to change the times and the law' but whose success was only of limited duration (7:25). For the author, omnipotence is the necessary concomitant of divinity, whereas the action of the earthly potentate is merely the display of human pride. What-ever the immediate gains of the latter, he himself is in the hands of the One who 'removes kings and sets up kings' (v. 21a).

As the book of Daniel is at pains to point out time and again, the wisdom by which God's servants act is not theirs but his. It is he who 'gives wisdom to the wise and knowledge to those who have understanding' (v. 21b). In keeping also with the overall tenor of the book, God is praised in the poem as the One who 'reveals deep and mysterious things' (v. 22a). These words might readily serve as an introduction to 2:36-46, but they are much more clearly a preparation for chs. 7 – 12. For man, the edge of darkness is the limit of sight beyond which he walks with uncer-tainty and often with fear. But not so for him who is the very creator of darkness himself: 'he knows what is in the darkness' and, moreover, 'the light dwells with him' (v. 22b). Here, in the contrasting of the two opposites, 'light' and 'darkness', as with 'good' and 'evil' in Gen. 2:17, is suggested the perfection and completeness of divine knowledge. That God is limited neither in might nor knowledge is central to the position and purpose of the author of Daniel. It is for him, and for those whom he ad-dressed, the sole source of comfort in the midst of oppression and persecution. This association of the deity with 'light' is common in biblical and related literature (see especially Ps. 36:10; Isa. 60:19-20; Wis. 7:24-26; 1 John 1:5-7). It is not surprising that in later Jewish thought the term used here for 'light' could be applied to the Messiah (Midrash *Lam.* Rab. i.51; T.B. *Sanh.* 98b).

The content of the poem is not at all alien to its present setting, though the overloading of the final verse (v. 23) does introduce a note of artificiality. Despite its many parallels with related literature it is a compelling liturgical composition, and there is no good reason to doubt its originality.

24-25 Alarmed by what he regarded as a rather peremptory act on the part of the king, Daniel now approaches Arioch. It is time for him to set in motion the course of events for which he has been chosen and prepared. It is time for the superiority of the God of Israel to be made known to all, not least to Nebuchadnezzar. The impression given of Arioch is that of a man reluctant to carry out his gruesome task. Whether he had faith in Daniel or not is not at all clear, but here at least is an opportunity for him to be released from the burden of the king's command. The alacrity with which he ushered Daniel into the royal presence is entirely understandable. The 6th-cent. setting of the story is underlined by the reference to Daniel as 'among the exiles from Judah' (v. 25). It is a feature of the story that Daniel, though a foreigner espousing an alien faith, is nevertheless readily accepted. There is no trace of any anti-Jewish or anti-Semitic sentiment. When friction does occur between Daniel and the Babylonians, or between his three companions and the local officials, it is the result, not of overt religious differences, but of a jealousy engendered by other causes.

26-30 The Nebuchadnezzar we meet at this point of the story is as anxious to find a solution to the matter as is Arioch. Consequently his question to Daniel is almost in the form of a plea. But it is important for him to be made aware of the limitations of human ability. To this extent Daniel is in accord with the Chaldeans (v. 11). But there is not complete agreement. Whereas they made claim that 'none can show it to the king except the gods', the author's reminder of their polytheism, Daniel responds to the king in terms of the faith and practice of his own tradition. What Daniel says of his own God, he says, too, of the God of the reader. It is not through the medium of the astrologer or the necromancer that the God of the Hebrews has made known his will but through the words of his servants, kings and prophets and wise men. Likewise, it is now through a chosen servant that he will make known the mystery of 'what will be in the latter days' (v. 28). The author stresses the source of Daniel's amazing ability rather than any accomplishment of the man himself. In similar circumstances, which were not far from the author's mind, Joseph had stood before the pharaoh of Egypt and disclaimed any personal prowess (Gen. 41:16). A new Joseph now stands before the king of Babylonia. Like the Joseph of old, Daniel accepts that it is the prerogative of a monarch to receive divine revelation; time has not eroded this understanding of the nature of kingship, but the king, as ever, is dependent for an interpretation on the good offices of a divinely appointed functionary.

The Hebrew Scriptures contain many examples of this royal dependence. One such is Isaiah's word to Hezekiah in 2 Kgs. 19:14-34. The monarch may be the most powerful man in the land, chosen of God like David, or used of God like Nebuchadnezzar (Dan. 1:1); nevertheless, the limits to his power and authority are strictly set. Kingship, whether native or foreign, is always treated in the Scriptures with due deference; it is an institution not without divine sanction, but it was never permitted either to usurp the power of God or to contravene his laws. Nebuchadnezzar, for all the power he might wield among and over his subjects, needs to be told 'what will be in the latter days.' This expression 'in the latter days' occurs again in 10:14 and with it we are introduced to the area of eschatology. The longing to know what is going to happen, what the future holds, is as natural as it is universal.

This story portrays Nebuchadnezzar as keen to look beyond to what is hidden from normal vision, but in this he is no more anxious than those for whom the tale was written, the harassed and persecuted Jews living in the days of Antiochus Epiphanes. In this respect, at least, the book of Daniel is aptly termed a 'tract for the times'. It had immediate significance for those second-century Jews whose hold on life grew more precarious with each passing day. It has less immediate yet undiminished significance for readers in all eras and stands in danger of losing that status only when it is subjected to undisciplined and overimaginative interpretation, when it is made to bear a weight for which it was not fashioned. To warn against the all-too-common misuse and abuse of this book is not to deny that it does provide us with some of the raw material of a 'theology of history'. But its usefulness as such is finely balanced. It is an important work, and it is understandable that men and women of faith will continually turn to it as they have in the past, but it must be emphasized that it is a limited work — limited by its initial purpose — and the finely adjusted balance may be easily upset.

Verses 27-30 bring together 'wisdom', 'eschatology', and 'apocalyptic'. Daniel is a 'wise man', the concern is with 'the latter days', and the language is veiled. The relationship of these must be taken seriously, but again a note of warning is in order. The wisdom of the book of Daniel is quite other than that of the book of Proverbs. Nor is there immediate rapport with other wisdom literature such as Job and Ecclesiastes. Its eschatology is embryonic. And, as apocalyptic, it stands close to the beginning of a movement that became more and more complex over the two centuries that immediately followed. When these three terms are used of this material, they must not be set loose from their immediate and circumscribing context.

31-35 The reader, like Nebuchadnezzar, has waited for this moment. At last the secret of the dream is to be revealed: 'You saw, O king, and behold, a great image [a tall statue]'. The description now follows. Its shape, though not its size, was that of a human being, with a head, chest, arms, and so on. Apart from its 'exceeding brightness' and a grotesque and frightening appearance, its most notable feature was the material from which it was made. It is this, the composition of the statue, that is of paramount importance. From head to toe it contained four distinct metals — gold, silver, bronze, and iron. But its most unusual feature was its feet. These consisted, not of one homogeneous substance, but of the unlikely mixture of iron and clay.

In describing the dream Daniel gives only the barest details, passing on quickly to where the interest of the story now lies, the fate of the statue. As with the giant Goliath of old (1 Sam. 17), one strategically aimed stone is sufficient to send the colossus crashing down. On this occasion, it is not the head that provides the point of greatest weakness, but the curious and unstable feet of iron and clay. Nor is the stone propelled by an arm wielding a slingshot. As it was 'cut out by no human hand', so it reached

its target through no human agency. The complete independence
of the destructive stone is asserted. It has required no human aid
to exist nor any human aid to act. Yet the result is eminently
effective and the telling of it is as brief as it is dramatic. First the
feet are smashed to pieces, followed in rapid succession by the
remainder of the statue, and the pulverised fragments become
like the chaff of the threshing floor, carried away by the wind
and lost forever. There is a reminder here of the fate of the ungodly in Ps. 1:4, though any connection is literary rather than
substantial. One might expect that the end of the image would
also signal the end of the dream. But that is not so. The stone
takes on a life of its own. It is not merely the agent of destruction,
but it occupies centre stage, and indeed expands to such proportions that it 'filled the whole earth' (v. 35). Any interpretation
must account not only for the statue, its composition and destruction, but for the stone as well. The lifeless statue has been obliterated; the stone remains.

Possibly the author knew of the existence of some ancient colossus and drew on this for the symbolism of the statue. He may
well have been aware of Iranian and Greek representations of
the cosmos in human form. Most commentators allude to the
various possibilities, but it has to be admitted that here we are
in the area of conjecture. Hartman offers the useful comment:
'But why seek to deprive our author of all originality?' (*The Book
of Daniel*, 146).

36-45 It is difficult to understand these verses without recourse
to the material of chs. 7 – 12, and in particular that of ch. 7 where
Daniel's vision of the four beasts is related. An obvious parallel
exists between the four metals and four kingdoms of ch. 2 and
the four beasts and four kingdoms of ch. 7. Furthermore, the
identification of the kingdoms is greatly facilitated by the substance of chs. 8 and 9.

Daniel's form of address to Nebuchadnezzar (v. 37) betrays
all the signs of accepted oriental court etiquette, but it is more
than that. It is consistent with the author's theological point of
view. The king is not a self-made man. Though Nebuchadnezzar
may be 'king of kings' (see Ezek. 26:7), he is so because his
kingdom has been given him by 'the God of heaven'. (In v. 37
Rashi translates 'a strong kingdom and power and honour.')

Flattering things are said of him in v. 38 where he is depicted as the lord of creation, but none more so than Daniel's assertion that he, Nebuchadnezzar, is 'the head of gold'. An earlier form of the story may have had as its subject successive reigns within the neo-Babylonian empire. In its extant second-century form, however, it has to do not with four kings but with four kingdoms. As v. 39 indicates, the line of Nebuchadnezzar (and his Babylonian successors) will not last forever. It will be replaced by a second and inferior kingdom, this in turn by a third, and that by a fourth. It is this fourth kingdom that moves to the centre of the picture. Little is said of the second and third, except to mention that the latter is of bronze. Presumably the former, i.e., the second kingdom, is of silver in keeping with the composition of the statue. With this the association of the four metals with four successive kingdoms or empires is complete. One further point that appears to have some part in the author's purpose is that this association is in descending order of value, i.e., from gold, to silver, to bronze, and finally to iron. This may be the author's judgment on these kingdoms, but it does not necessarily rank them in importance or in strength if we are to take seriously what is said of the fourth in v. 40.

This depiction of kingdoms in terms of metals is by no means novel, though it has no strict parallel. Writing in the early 8th cent. B.C.E., the Greek Hesiod used a similar descending order of values to pronounce judgment on the moral decline of his own time. Through a sequence of Five Ages man has moved from the race of gold to the iron generation of Hesiod's contemporaries. The suggestiveness of such an image is not difficult to appreciate, and doubtless in many variations it was taken up by later authors. Whatever its origin it is present in its own particular form in Daniel 2 as the central feature of Nebuchadnezzar's dream. The important question is now one of identification. All that the storyteller has permitted the reader to know is that the first kingdom is the Babylonian, of which Nebuchadnezzar was the fitting representative. On a strict reading of what is known of the history of the ancient Near East the three empires that in turn succeeded the neo-Babylonian would have to be the Persian, Greek (divided after the death of Alexander the Great), and Roman.

This interpretation has found wide acceptance among commentators both early and recent. It is to be found consistently in

the Talmud (e.g., *'Abod. Zar.* 2b) and among medieval Jewish
commentators such as R. Saadiah Gaon, R. Moshe ben Maimon,
and R. Moshe ben Nachman. This lead has been followed, in the
main, within traditional Judaism. Two factors in particular give
support to this thesis. The first is that the Talmudic and Mid-
rashic authors were themselves aware of the postponement of the
longed-for messianic kingdom of God, and very much aware of
the ferocious power of Rome to whose control they were subject.
It was Rome that destroyed the Second Temple in 70 C.E., and
Rome that put down so brutally the Bar Kokhba revolt in 135
C.E. and drove the Jews from their land. Second, as time passed
it was not difficult for the religious power, the Christian Church,
to be substituted for the secular power, Rome, for had not the
boundaries of the two become all but contiguous? It is salutary
for Christian readers, especially those who wish to interpret the
fourth kingdom as some extant despotic and antireligious state,
to have this word from a modern Jewish commentator:

> The powerless orphan adopted by the mighty empire, orig-
> inally by Emperor Constantine I and later by his succes-
> sors, grew up to utilize its unique position as state religion
> of the great empire and moved on to a period of unprece-
> dented growth. Its power, whether temporal or spiritual,
> eclipses that of kingdoms and empires. Thus throughout
> our exile, the fourth kingdom is represented by the Chris-
> tian church, conceived of, despite all its diverse forms, as
> one unit. (R. H. Goldwurm, *Daniel*, 59)

Early Christian exegesis tended to be influenced by the earlier
Jewish identification of the fourth kingdom with the secular Roman empire. Despite the prima facie strength of this position,
however, it has been largely abandoned. The most commonly
accepted schema of the nation is Babylonia, Media, Persia, and
Greece. The arguments in favour of this ordering are:

(i) It is required by the plain sense of ch. 11, which is, as
Montgomery observed, the 'one sure and definite bit of
secular history in the book' (*The Book of Daniel*, 59).

(ii) It is in keeping with a schema known to Herodotus
(5th cent. B.C.E.) and Ctesias (4th cent. B.C.E.) where the
order is Assyria, Media, and Persia. For the author of Daniel the immediate concern is not with the Assyrians but

with the power that brought about the Exile, the Babylonians. He has not confused the traditional order but has deliberately altered it to suit his own purpose.

In doing so he has created a difficulty by placing the Medes subsequent to the Babylonians and preceding the Persians, whereas historical records make it clear that Media had been absorbed into the Persian empire of Cyrus before the collapse of Babylonia. (The artificiality of the author's schema and the perpetuation of a historical inaccuracy in no way detract from the message of the book.)

(iii) It is possible that the author and, for that matter, popular opinion were influenced by certain passages from the prophets, namely, Isa. 13:17 and Jer. 51:11, 28-29, where Media is directed by God to take part in the destruction of Babylon. This would necessitate the order Babylonia, Media, Persia, and Greece.

(iv) In the long run the whole thrust of the book of Daniel as a Word of God spoken to faithful Jews who were themselves in the midst of oppression and persecution demands such an interpretation. To project that into an unreal situation in some historically remote time is to fail to come to grips with the central purpose of the book, and is in danger of emptying it of any real claim to canonicity. Yet one must go on to say that the initially conditioned interpretation of Scripture does not exhaust the possibilities. When these words are read within the context of a believing community they may take on new and added significance.

The fourth kingdom is portrayed as having the strength of iron and the ability to crush and destroy. But that it has singular weakness is suggested by the description of its feet (and toes) as consisting of iron and ceramic. Verses 41-43 betray signs of reworking and read less than smoothly; however, the point is sufficiently clear. The incompatible components of the lower region of the statue denote a division within the fourth kingdom itself. This is borne out by our knowledge of the times. The two parts of the Greek or Macedonian empire of Alexander the Great, here referred to by implication, are the Ptolemaic which centred on Egypt and the Seleucid which centred on Syria. So far as any 2nd-cent. resident of Jerusalem was concerned, these were the two powers within the Diadochi (see also Dan. 11:3-4) established on the death of Alexander in 323 B.C.E. which influenced his own life and those of his compatriots. The narrow strip of land which included the province of Judea was under the control of one or the other for almost a century and a half. First the Ptolemaic dynasty was in the ascendancy, thus forging a link between Jerusalem and Alexandria that in time produced the Septuagint. With the victory of Antiochus II at the Battle of Paneas in 198 B.C.E. the hegemony over the disputed area passed to the Seleucids. Unsuccessful attempts were made by means of intermarriage to bring the two contending powers to peaceful agreement, and these are no doubt alluded to in v. 43. As such this verse anticipates the fuller references in 11:6 and 17.

Our attention thus far has been focussed on the fourth kingdom and its subsidiaries; it must now be directed towards the fifth, for in it lies the hope for the future. Four specific things are said of it:

(a) it will be set up by the God of heaven,

(b) it will be indestructible and therefore everlasting,

(c) its sovereignty will never be passed on to another people, and

(d) it will put an end to all the kingdoms previously referred to.

The destruction of the four kingdoms is brought about by the stone that 'was cut from a mountain by no human hand' (v. 45). In the dream this statement was expanded on. The stone itself 'became a great mountain and filled the whole earth' (v. 35). Presumably this spatial description of the fifth kingdom is taken up in the reference to it as 'everlasting'. The note of promise to those hemmed in by powers not of their own choosing is that their degradation and suffering will come to an end, and that end is in the hands of God. The kingdoms to which in succession they have been subject will not be replaced by another of the same kind and similar inclination but by a divinely ordained regime in which they themselves will be sovereign. Though the unequivocal statement of Israel's inheritance must await the vision of ch. 7 there is little doubt that the words 'nor shall its sovereignty be left to another people' hold the sure word of liberation. It is also indisputable that what is being spoken of is not a kingdom beyond this world but one that is securely fastened to earth. In this respect at least, the apocalypticism of ch. 2 is decidedly early. Whether it is to be interpreted messianically or not is another matter. Lacocque notes the absence of what he terms 'messianic features' but goes on to comment: 'The stone, mentioned in vv. 34-5 and interpreted in v. 44 as the Kingdom of God, belongs to the Messianic sphere' (*The Book of Daniel*, 52).

This argument, however, requires more than mere reference to episodes in which the word 'stone' or 'rock' appears to substantiate it, even when those episodes relate to the lives of great Hebrews of the past such as Jacob and Joseph. There is a sense in which the term 'messianic' may be used so generally that it signifies nothing more than an association with some future event. In that case it loses all possible significance and would better be replaced by a suitable synonym. It is a different matter when the specifically technical and presumably personal title 'messianic' is used. Confident use of this term requires clear and unequivocal support. As a description of the content of the texts before us it is far too ambitious and, consequently, misleading. Rashi may well be correct when he asserts that the divine kingdom will be governed by the Messiah, but nothing in Daniel 2 supports such a claim.

46-49 Daniel's assurance to the king in v. 45 that 'The dream is certain, and its interpretation is sure', is accepted without demur. Nebuchadnezzar's attitude to Daniel is more than respectful. The author of the story has him do obeisance before the Jewish hero and, in so doing, introduces not only a curious twist but a genuine embarrassment. That more than an expression of civility is involved is patently clear from the technical sacrificial terms that are used in the Aramaic text. What possible explanation can there be for this presentation of the faithful Daniel receiving, apparently without protest, the worshipful homage of a fellow human being? Porteous suggests that a note of humour may be involved, while Hartman, following Montgomery, takes up a parallel experience in the life of Alexander the Great who explained his homage to the high priest of Jerusalem, not as worship of the man, but of the God whom he represented. Still another possible explanation is that here Daniel epitomises the

Jewish people who, on behalf of their God, will receive the sub-
mission of the nations (see Lacocque). Rashi seeks a way out of
the difficulty by implying in his translation that Nebuchadnezzar
intended to offer sacrifices to Daniel but the latter prevented him.
This places an unbearable burden on the word usually translated
'commanded' (RSV, Lacocque) or 'ordered' (Hartman). Some
Talmudic texts accept the difficulty and are not slow to apportion
blame to the great man Daniel. And that is an interesting point.
Hebrew heroes, whether in the OT or in later writings, are never
exempt from the word of critical judgment. How many of the
great names of this tradition — Moses, David, Solomon, and now
Daniel — are literally cut down to size! Heroes they were, to be
sure; but never demigods beyond reproof. Always they remained
human, and the weakness of their humanity was never simply
glossed over.

Nebuchadnezzar's confession that the God of Daniel is truly
'God of gods and Lord of kings, and a revealer of mysteries
. . .' (v. 47) is the climactic point of the chapter. It is as unnec-
essary to posit that the king became a convert to the Jewish faith
as it is to canvass the possibility that we are here dealing with
history. The story of the dream and its interpretation require no
historical setting. Figures of the past lend themselves to the purpose of the author whose primary aim has been to secure just
such a confession as that made by Nebuchadnezzar.

After Daniel reveals the king's dream, it is to be expected that
he should be amply rewarded. The author had access to the tale
of Joseph's elevation in the court of pharaoh. For a similar service
Daniel must receive a similar honour. What is a little surprising
is that at his request Daniel's three companions should receive
such advancement. Perhaps their introduction at this point is to
provide a link with what is to follow in ch. 3. While Daniel remains in the king's court Shadrach, Meshach, and Abednego go
further afield to attend to the everyday matters of government.

While ch. 2 does have many features in common with its immediate context, and may be rightly termed a 'court-tale', it has
other features more closely aligned to the material of the second
half of the book. A rereading of this chapter in light of the treatment of chs. 7 – 12 may prove rewarding.

OBEDIENCE AND SUFFERING
Daniel 3:1-30

Some introductory remarks are necessary before the text is examined more closely. Chapter 3 has many points in common with ch. 6. Each has to do with rivalry between jealous Babylonian officials and quickly promoted foreigners in the court of the monarch. Parallels, at least in part, are to be found in the stories of Joseph and Esther. In ch. 3 as well as in ch. 6 the heroes are put in great danger; destruction should follow, but through divine intervention this is avoided. The movement is from scurrilous accusation to unjust punishment, and from imminent death to miraculous rescue.

It is a matter for regret that biblical stories of this nature have so often been regarded as having a peculiar fascination for younger readers and consequently have been relegated to the Sunday School or its equivalent. The tacit assumption is that there is not very much in this material beyond a good story well told. This being the case, the place for such stories, given their element of the miraculous, is not with serious-minded adults but with those for whom they will have an immediate and probably exhilarating appeal. One objection that may be levelled at this common practice is that, though the horrific nature of some of the stories is somewhat tempered by the dramatic and thrilling escape of the heroes, the plots are nevertheless quite gruesome. A fiery furnace prepared for the burning of human beings, and a pit of lions whose grizzly purpose is the ravaging of a defenceless man, may not be the best introductory material for the study of the Bible at a junior level. But a far more serious objection is that the familiarity attained with these stories at an early age tends to insulate the mature reader from the serious nature and purpose of the stories, and leads to the adoption of the attitude that they are not really deserving of serious attention.

As a partial correction to this view the following might be noted. Both chs. 3 and 6 are essential components of the canonical book of Daniel. They are two in a series of stories the purpose of which was on the one hand to underscore the lengths to which the course of political despotism could run, and on the other, and more importantly, to assure the faithful that adherence to principle is to be preferred to apostasy, even though martyrdom may well be the outcome. That this book received what may be called canonical status shortly after the period for which it was prepared and adopted is witness to its ongoing relevance for a people who recognised that its words of censure and of encouragement were not restricted to any one circumstance nor to any one time. It is with that thought in mind that these stories must be approached, for they have nurtured the faith of the people of God in dark and desperate times.

What we know of the despotism and cruelty of ancient times, with its less sophisticated practices, might lead us to believe that brutality and genocide were no more than the expression of mankind's infancy, of a world that knew no better, that was given over to barbarity. But a closer reading of the available documentation indicates that that was not the case. Those early times were no more barbaric than any other period of history. If we leave aside for the moment the difficult question of the initial provenance of these stories and attend to the Hellenistic period in which they received their present form, we will be reminded that for every rapacious Antiochus Epiphanes there were a hundred scholars and artists of noble character and of lasting importance in whose debt we all remain. Perhaps that should be a comfort to us; in the midst of darkness the light continues to shine. But it is no real comfort. If on the one hand we applaud the spread of Greek culture by means of the academy and gymnasium, we must ask, on the other, how such flowering of the human mind and spirit could be attended by the tacit acceptance of behaviour and policies that were destructive not only of other cultures but of other human beings. The 'fiery furnace' may be a literary invention and may have had no exact equivalent, but it is too uncomfortably close to the maniacal expressions of ethnic hatred of our own day to be passed over lightly. The cadences of Greek poetry could be heard not far from the dungeons of Antiochus Epiphanes, and the strains of the Bach motet were carried on the same breeze as the smoke from Auschwitz. There is little distance between the Fiery Furnace and the Holocaust. These two monstrous events — the one literary fiction, the other unbelievable fact — are both expressions of a demonic attempt to silence the spirit of faith and, with it, the voice of God. Chapter 3 of the book of Daniel is not simply a story for children.

1-7 The initial focus of the chapter is on a huge but ill-proportioned 'image of gold' constructed by order of King Nebuchadnezzar. Apart from its composition and dimensions, ninety feet by nine, little information is given about it. Nothing in the text would indicate whether it is or is not a statue, or whether it has or does not have a human form. It is because of its proportions that the view has been advanced that it may have been a stele (a commemorative pillar or upright slab). The text's silence may be penetrated, however, and a different solution reached. It is not likely that the author would have left the story in its present seemingly uninformative shape if there had not been some means of satisfying the curiosity of his contemporaries. For an answer to the question that must have been as obvious in his time as it is in ours, we are driven back to the content of ch. 2. That the connection between these two chapters is artificial does not militate against this possibility. Indeed, it may enhance it. The artificiality of the sudden and unexpected appearance of Shadrach, Meshach, and Abednego (2:49), the heroes of ch. 3, serves to underline the one vital link between the two chapters and obviates the need for any description of the image beyond what is given. If this is so, the image is a statue, and it is a statue of Nebuchadnezzar himself. It may be surmised that it was the author's intention to present the king in the following way. (It should be borne in mind that in stories of this type the intention of the author is paramount. The search for historical support, beyond the mere incidentals, is as futile as it is unwarranted.) The Nebuchadnezzar of ch. 2, through the good graces of the divinely inspired Daniel, has become the possessor of two important pieces of information. In the dream (2:32, 38) he is the head of gold, but important though his kingdom thus signified may be, it will be superseded by another. The Nebuchadnezzar of the book of Daniel, despite his enthusiasm for the interpretation of the dream, is not the kind of monarch who would view with equanimity the ultimate disintegration of his dynasty, for that is what the interpretation must point to. Like Antiochus Epiphanes of a later day he intended 'to change the times', to alter history's course. The massive statue of gold might not hold back his own physical demise, but it would serve to perpetuate his memory and that of his line, and so satisfy his pride. That the statue was of a deified Nebuchadnezzar was advanced by the first Christian commentator on the book of Daniel, the priest Hippolytus, writing from Rome in the first decade of the 3rd cent. C.E. This may be the most obvious solution but it is not necessarily incorrect for being so.

A more or less exact location, the plain of Dura, is introduced to suggest both historical and geographical verisimilitude. Jewish tradition has asserted and recent commentators have accepted that Dura ('a walled place' in Babylonian) was in the region south of Babylon near Hilla. It was natural that anything as important as a newly constructed statue of the reigning monarch should have a fitting service of dedication, the more so in light of the role it was destined to play. The invitation list for such an occasion was necessarily a lengthy one including, for reasons of protocol if for no other, every conceivable category of officialdom from ministers of state to provincial chiefs. But the list has an importance beyond its length. The terms used for four of the delineated groups, and possibly for a fifth, are Persian. This is no clear indication of provenance nor of the date of original composition. It may be that the author in employing Persian words here and elsewhere was doing no more than avoiding blatant anachronistic usage. The matter is complicated still further by the terms used for the various musical instruments in v. 5. Three of the six are loanwords from Greek. Here again this does not allow making unassailable statements as to dating. It does not necessarily suggest composition during or later than the time of Alexander the Great. Although it is readily agreed that Hellenization both in language and in culture followed hard on his conquests, it is contrary to what is known of cultural influence and language-borrowing to assert that these are necessarily present only as a result of territorial expansion. However, when the above points are considered and when other factors are noted, not least the theological and religious stance of the book as a whole, the evident purpose as a message of encouragement and hope to a persecuted people, and the language, vocabulary, and style, what may be ruled out is the possibility of composition in the 6th cent. B.C.E. The dating of individual chapters within the first part of the book, i.e., chs. 1 – 6, is a difficult task and not accompanied by unanimous scholarly agreement. But the weight of evidence as well as of erudite opinion favours a final production in the 2nd cent. B.C.E. of material that circulated as individual stories in a more or less identifiable form in the two centuries prior to that date.

The herald's proclamation in v. 4 is meant to be all-embracing. Nebuchadnezzar was to all intents and purposes the conqueror of the world. The region under his control was immense, and beyond its borders was only the unknown or the unknowable. Many 'peoples, nations, and languages' were subject to him, and as a result of his deportation policy, a practice not unlike that of the earlier Assyrian power, Babylon itself and its environs had become distinctly cosmopolitan. But the multiple listing of addresses is more than that; it is part of the art of the storyteller; so, too, is the constant repetition of them. By such means, and in keeping with ancient protocol, the preeminence of the king is demonstrated. The author goes along with Nebuchadnezzar's estimation of himself and makes every effort to maintain it.

With the erection of the image and the performance of the dedication ceremony, the real drama of the story is about to begin. This proclamation permits no exceptions. Those who refuse to prostrate themselves before the image and worship it will 'immediately be cast into a burning fiery furnace' (v. 6). The Jewish reader, certainly one living in the 2nd cent., knew what this meant. He knew that it would be only a matter of time before one or more of his own people would be arraigned before the authorities and consigned to the fire. Who would it be? And how would it happen?

8-12 Those who bring the accusation are 'certain Chaldeans' (v. 8). Here the term is being used, not in a wider ethnic sense, but in the sense encountered in 2:2. The accusation appears to arise from professional jealousy and, although it is leveled against 'the Jews', is not to be understood as inherently anti-Semitic. That it may now be seen to presage unparalleled human tragedy requires the experience of nearly two thousand years of Christianity. In its initial context it arose from feelings equally base but nevertheless much more circumscribed and much more controllable. The Jews accused by the Chaldeans in this story are singled out because of the advancement they had received at the hands of the king himself, but no doubt there was a tacit warning which the alert reader would not have allowed to pass unnoticed. There is a measure of insubordination in the words of the accusers to Nebuchadnezzar. The king is curtly reminded of his beneficence towards Shadrach, Meshach, and Abednego. These, say the Chaldeans to their overlord, are men 'whom you have appointed over the affairs of the province of Babylon' (v. 12; see also 2:49).

The accusation is threefold. Shadrach, Meshach, and Abednego are culpable, so it is claimed, on three counts: disobedience of the king's order (they 'pay no heed to you'), refusal to worship the golden image, and failure to serve Nebuchadnezzar's gods. The last of these appears to be somewhat extraneous and is not directly related to the royal proclamation. Because of its general nature it is possible that it is a 2nd-cent. addition. There were no doubt a considerable number of these in chs. 1–6, few of which are readily identifiable. Broad religious proscriptions of that nature were in effect during the time of Antiochus IV and quite certainly from 167 to 165 B.C.E. On the other hand, under the Babylonians and Persians there was no evidence of any official interference with Jewish worship or other religious practices. Persian policy was markedly enlightened, and early friction between Babylonians and exiled Jews was more popular than official and confined to taunting jibes such as those found in the exilic Psalm 137. Religion and politics could as yet be kept apart. To suggest that the enforced worship of Nebuchadnezzar's image runs counter to this assessment is to historicize what is in fact no more than a story and to miss the point of the story itself.

The three Jews were easy targets for the accusation, as would have been any of their compatriots. To remain loyal to Torah and to be innocent of breach of the royal proclamation was not possible. The commandment in Exod. 20:3-5 (and Deut. 5:7-9) permits no qualification: 'You shall have no other gods before me. You shall not make for yourself a graven image . . . you shall not bow down to them or serve them . . . .' The history of Israel has been played out in terms of this commandment. It is at the very heart of Hebrew faith.

13-18 The response of Shadrach, Meshach, and Abednego (the Babylonian conferred names are used throughout this chapter) is a further act of defiance, but for them it has its counterpart in Nebuchadnezzar's own defiance of the one true God. His proclamation strikes at the roots of monotheism. In the story he is the representative of ungodly power, of a human pride that cannot tolerate the exclusive claim of a monotheistic faith. George Steiner writes of 'the singularity, the brain-hammering strangeness of the monotheistic idea' (*Bluebeard's Castle*). From Nebuchadnezzar to Antiochus Epiphanes, and from the Emperor Julian to modern times, this clamp on the human desire for ultimate freedom has been resisted and ridiculed. Monotheists have but one choice, and one only, and having made it they leave themselves with no other god to deploy against the One they have chosen or been chosen by. The attraction of polytheism is that it widens every choice; it imposes no limitation. It would have saved the lives of Shadrach and his two companions without the necessity of a miracle.

It is to Nebuchadnezzar's credit, furious though he must have been, that he eschewed acting merely on the word of the informers. The accused themselves were summoned to his presence and given an opportunity to affirm or deny the charge brought against them. This personal and immediate confrontation with the king has a clear purpose in the story. It is one thing to defy a decree in the relative obscurity of the gathered multitude; it is quite another to continue that defiance face to face with the personification of authority and the embodiment of power. We may assume that the point of this part of the story is that if the faithful Jew is to demonstrate his loyalty to the one true God he must be prepared to see it through step by step with ever increasing risk to his own life. From the initial act of confession, or in its negative projection, defiance, and martyrdom, there is an ascending scale of temptations, of opportunities to recant.

The threat of death by burning is again made, this time by Nebuchadnezzar. Moreover, it is accompanied by the king's confident prediction of the impossibility of divinely mediated deliverance. In short, what god can rescue from the hand of the divine

Nebuchadnezzar himself (v. 15)? For the author and his people the blasphemy of such an assertion is not so much the shallowness of its human boastfulness as the bankruptcy of its theology. Nebuchadnezzar's bold claim enshrouds the fragility of polytheism, which pits one god against another. We are reminded of the less veiled but derisive appraisal of the Babylonian pantheon in Isa. 44:9-17, particularly v. 17: 'And the rest of it he makes into a god, his idol; and falls down to it and worships it; he prays to it and says, "Deliver me, for thou art my god!" ' (See also Isa. 41:19-20 and 46:1-2.)

The reply of the three Jews, as it is translated according to the cantillation of the MT, borders on the disrespectful. This would be quite out of keeping with the author's portrayal of the attitude of Jewish subjects to foreign monarchs throughout the book. It is most unlikely that the correct translation has three appointed officials of Nebuchadnezzar address him by the use of his name alone. The tenor of the reply, however, leaves no doubt as to where they stand. Their action, they claim, speaks for itself. What they add to the opening sentence is not at all clear, as is indicated by the addition in the footnotes to the RSV of two other possible renderings. Hartman introduces a further possibility (*Daniel*, 155). An examination of the chief contending translations leads to the following possible interpretations of vv. 17 and 18:

(i) If God is able to save them, he will do so (RSV footnote).

(ii) If God who is able to deliver them should choose not to do so . . . (RSV text).

(iii) If there is a God able to save them, then he will do so. But in the event that there is no such God . . . (Hartman).

Hartman's translation may imply a movement between 'god' and 'God', but as it stands, it can be taken in the sense of a questioning of the existence not only of a 'god' able to save but of 'God' as such, and is therefore a most unlikely rendering in this context. Interpretation (i) is to be rejected on the grounds that any questioning of the ability of God to come to the rescue of his own faithful servants is out of place in a book which seeks to present the God of Israel as Lord of history. Interpretation (ii), i.e., the one based on the RSV text, is to be preferred. It is grammatically and syntactically possible; it confesses the ability of God to rescue the three; but it acknowledges that it may not be the will of God to do so. So far as this latter point is concerned, it is in keeping with the assertion of Ps. 115:3: 'Our God is in the heavens; he does whatever he pleases'.

Neither here nor anywhere else in the Hebrew Scriptures is there an underwritten guarantee that every faithful Jew will be delivered from the consequences of his or her devotion to God should circumstances produce a threat to that person's life. Practical experience alone would have prevented the author of the book of Daniel from making any such claim. Any belief so neatly stated would have lasted no longer than its first exception. No doubt the ways of God in matters like this were as much a mystery and a puzzle to the author as they are to us. The experience of Daniel in ch. 6 must be similarly interpreted.

19-23   The second chance offered the three heroes was not theirs by right but an act of condescension on the part of the king. It is not difficult to imagine that Nebuchadnezzar experiences a sense of disappointment because of the reply he has received. As is so often the case where the offer of help seemingly is arbitrarily rejected, the attitude towards the offenders changes from one of pleading to one of downright fury. Consistency, if nothing else, would have demanded that the king carry out the threatened execution, but now, his plea having been spurned, he is portrayed as entering into it with great enthusiasm. Regal commands are flashed out in several directions. The furnace is to be heated to seven times its usual temperature and a number of particularly strong men are called to take hold of and bind the three. Nebuchadnezzar has decided to take no chances. Perhaps the fire at ordinary heat would have been no match for the God of Shadrach, Meshach, and Abednego, but surely this excessive heat will keep him at bay. Perhaps it is in the divine plan to wrest them out of his hand, but this phalanx of burly henchmen should foil any such attempt. If the God of the Jews was going to intervene, Nebuchadnezzar was determined to thwart him at every turn. The polytheism of the king could entertain a contest between equals. The monotheism of the author allows him to make sport of his enemies. The story is not without its element of satire. Meanwhile, the three men, in what would appear to be their official regalia, are hurled into the flaming furnace with the un-

expected immediate result of the scorching to death of those who
carried out the king's order. Neither here nor on the basis of the
like situation at the close of ch. 6 is it legitimate to draw doctrinal
conclusions.

In the LXX the story is interrupted at this point by the Prayer
of Azariah, which is followed first by an addition to the story
itself and then by the Hymn of the Three Young Men. A discussion of this material is beyond the scope of this commentary, as
is deliberation on its status, i.e., whether it is rightfully to be
reckoned as canonical or otherwise. The reader is referred to the
work of C. A. Moore, *Daniel, Esther, and Jeremiah: The Additions.*

24-30 By a means which the author does not divulge, Nebuchadnezzar is able to approach the blazing furnace and peer into
it. He is startled by what he sees. The intended victims have not
been burned to cinders. Rather, their bonds have been shed and
they are walking around, completely unharmed. What is more,
the king sees not only the three offenders but a fourth figure, the
appearance of whom, he claims, 'is like a son of the gods' (v. 25).
At this point it is necessary to resist the temptation to provide
a christological interpretation. What are we then to understand
by the description of this enigmatic figure? A number of times in
the Hebrew Scriptures we find the formula 'sons of God', e.g.,
Gen. 6:2; Job 1:6; and 38:7. In each of these cases the word in
the construct state, i.e., the first word in the genitival expression,
is in the plural form. It is commonly accepted that what are
being referred to in these instances are nonhuman, semidivine
beings which constitute a kind of heavenly court. The task allotted to these 'sons of God' is the service of the deity and the
carrying out of his will. In Hebrew the word in the singular is
ben, and in Aramaic, *bar.* The most common translation of these
words in English is 'son', and in most cases that suits the context
admirably. The word *ben* (or *bar*) does not necessarily imply a
generic relationship, however. It may do no more than denote
membership within a certain group or classification. It can be
said of a boy that he is 'ben-fourteen', i.e., he is fourteen years
of age. That is the group, the age category, to which he belongs.
In the text before us the classification is determined by the final
word of the expression. In the RSV this is rendered 'God', but
this is not the only possibility. In fact, it may be misleading

36

simply to translate it in that way. A better English word would be 'divine', for this is the classification alluded to. The combination of the relational word and the classification word in v. 25 suggests the rendering 'a divine being'. In other words, what Nebuchadnezzar saw was a heavenly messenger sent to carry out God's will, namely, the rescue of the three young men.

The point of the story is that the man of faith, who holds fast to what God requires of him, will not be left alone. He is not simply abandoned to alien and destructive forces. We do the story less than justice if we fail to interpret it within its own context, or if we go beyond its main theme by erecting on the basis of its particulars a general principle that might hold for all time.

Having in mind certain expressions used of Daniel elsewhere in the book (4:8, 9, 18; 5:12; 6:3), Lacocque makes the interesting comment that Daniel, who receives no mention in this story, 'is perhaps not so far from chapter 3 as we might have believed. The one who substitutes for the absent Daniel is "like a son of God/the gods" ' (*Daniel*, 66). The 15th-cent. Jewish commentator Abarbanel more explicitly suggested a like identification.

In calling them from the furnace Nebuchadnezzar describes the three as 'servants of the Most High God' (v. 26), the author's first indication that the king is a changed man. Further evidence of this is yet to come. The title itself appears from time to time on the lips of non-Israelites, indicating perhaps, in an oblique way, that so far as the OT is concerned it is a borrowed divine epithet (see Gen. 14:18-20 and Num. 24:16). The king is quick to point out to the rescued trio that their trust in God, the substance of their reply to him in vv. 17-18, has been vindicated. They have emerged unscathed, the subjects of a miraculous deliverance wrought by their God. The effect on Nebuchadnezzar is little short of miraculous itself. The story opens with the king erecting an image of himself and proclaiming its compulsory worship. It closes with another decree, to the effect that any calumny spoken against the God of Shadrach, Meshach, and Abednego will be punished with a fearful death and the property of the offender obliterated. This second decree does not go as far as its counterpart in ch. 6, but it does stand as recognition of the incomparable delivering power of the God of Israel (v. 29). From the lips of the great Nebuchadnezzar that is praise indeed, and, in the author's purpose, a great source of encouragement to the people of God.

For their part the three heroes receive further promotion (v. 30), and with that they fade out of the book of Daniel, but not out of the traditions of their own people. There is an honoured place for them in Mattathias's catalogue of great men in 1 Maccabees:

> Elijah because of his great zeal for the law was taken up into heaven; Hananiah, Azariah, and Mishael believed and were saved from the fire. (1 Macc. 2:58-59)

CHAPTER 4

THE KINGDOM OF THE MOST HIGH

Daniel 4:1-34

The message of this chapter may simply be stated as 'the mastery of destiny'. The story is woven around two thoughts in particular which, in the form of two texts, serve as constant reminders of the author's purpose:

— the Most High rules the kingdom of men (vv. 17, 25, and 32)

— those who walk in pride he is able to abase (v. 37; cf. v. 17)

1-3 The first three verses appear in the MT as the closing verses of ch. 3. Here, although chapter divisions have come to assist us greatly in our reading and understanding of the Hebrew Scriptures, they are not a feature of the earliest Hebrew and Aramaic texts. They are not of Masoretic origin but appear for the first time in Christian texts of medieval times. If any departure from the traditional arrangement is necessitated, it is a departure from a relatively recent tradition only. What, then, is the proper place of vv. 1-3? They might serve as an epilogue to the story of the miraculous deliverance of the three young men or as a preface to what follows in ch. 4. Though they are not out of context if they are made to serve the former purpose, all in all they appear to be somewhat more closely related to the context of ch. 4. Perhaps the appearance of 'to all peoples, nations, and languages' in 4:1 could have strongly suggested their position within the MT. It is clear, however, that ch. 4 is cast in the form of an epistle from King Nebuchadnezzar, and these terms signify the groups for whom the epistle is intended. The formal language of the greeting, the succinct statement of purpose, together with the sender's name, are known epistolary forms and have their close parallels in both secular and biblical literature. The 'signs and wonders' to which the king refers in v. 2, and again in the doxology (v. 3), might well serve as a reminder of the great deeds of God demonstrated in the previous chapter. The form of ch. 4, however, demands that they be seen as anticipatory references to an experience that will befall Nebuchadnezzar himself. Certain key expressions of the doxology itself bear a striking resemblance to the words of Ps. 145:13a.

4-18 The central character of this story is Nebuchadnezzar. Apart from Daniel he is the dominating character of the first four chapters. It is the king who is the unifying factor in these early stories, for he alone appears in all four. Daniel was nowhere on the scene when his three companions were undergoing their horrific experience.

The picture we are given of Nebuchadnezzar in v. 4 is that of the successful and satisfied potentate, not unlike that of the rich landowner in the parable of Luke 12:15-21. The king is at the pinnacle of achievement. He could well afford to be 'at ease' in his house, for his kingdom was indeed prospering. The underlying Aramaic word suggests the sense of 'flourishing'. For him nothing could be better. This is the other necessary ingredient of the picture. Both personally and politically all was well. What could possibly disturb this scene of tranquility and confidence? This is the situation of the Nebuchadnezzar of the storyteller, and it is well borne out by the historical record. There is no question that Nebuchadnezzar deserves to be reckoned among the great rulers of the ancient world. If a Jewish writer had good cause to see in him the villainous conqueror of his own people and the destroyer of the Holy City, he also had the constant reminder of the prophetic writings that Nebuchadnezzar had been the instrument of the God of Israel. The book of Daniel displays a discernible and understandable ambivalence toward Nebuchadnezzar. The writer of chs. 2 and 4 must also have been aware of that word of warning addressed to a previous instrument of God in Isa. 10:15:

> Shall the axe vaunt itself over him
>   who hews with it;
> or the saw magnify itself against him
>   who wields it?

For his part, Nebuchadnezzar might well view the future with equanimity. The storyteller knows better. The intruder on the scene of royal tranquility was something beyond the control even of the monarch. For all the ingenuity and accomplishment of man, king or commoner, he is unable to stifle what seems to be the most innocuous of human experiences, the dream. Its effect on Nebuchadnezzar was one of fear and alarm, and these emotions gathered in intensity as he lay pondering what had just happened to him. The lowest ranking among his servants would have been able to inform him that the dark hours of the night are not the domain of rationality. The contrast between his state of mind in v. 4 and in v. 5 is dramatic. The storyteller has effected it in just two short sentences.

Unlike the ordinary person left to his own meagre resources, in such a circumstance Nebuchadnezzar was able to summon to his aid all the professional interpreters of the realm. These 'wise men of Babylon' (v. 6) have already been openly discredited and their appearance now seems almost superfluous. The proven Daniel might have expedited matters considerably. In reading these stories, however, it is unwise to carry over all the details of one to another. The method of the storyteller is eclectic and peculiarly his own, designed not to give details of happenings within the court, but rather to use the names of historical personages to convey a message to his people.

The various categories of soothsayers now brought in before the king differ slightly from those listed in 2:2 and include one group, the 'astrologers', previously mentioned in 2:27. This time the task set them is not nearly as difficult as the one already faced. Then they were expected to reveal both dream and interpretation. On this occasion Nebuchadnezzar relates the dream and seeks only its interpretation. Even this they are unable to provide, and so the Babylonian wise men move out of the story as quickly as they entered it. Their lack of ability draws no criticism from the king. There are no threats as in ch. 2. The reason is that here these men have been used merely to prepare the way for Daniel. In ch. 2 the various protagonists are far more important to the story than they are in ch. 4. Here the interest is overwhelmingly with the content of the dream and its interpretation, i.e., with the message. Important though he is, even Daniel moves in and out of the story with ease. There is in this tale neither reward nor preferment for the hero himself. It is Nebuchadnezzar who occupies centre stage, who offers the hymn of praise, and who makes all the profound theological statements because he, in a sense, is the bearer of the message.

In ch. 1 we were informed that Ashpenaz renamed Daniel Belteshazzar (1:7; cf. 5:12). This conferred name is used only once in ch. 2, namely, v. 26, but is commonly found in ch. 4, particularly on the lips of Nebuchadnezzar. This preferential usage is underlined when the king refers to Daniel as 'he who was named Belteshazzar after the name of my god' (v. 8). It is of little consequence that etymologically this description is unsound. What is striking is the bond that the author appears to construct between the king and the 'chief of the magicians' (v. 9). It is no reflection on the devotion and loyalty of Daniel the Jew that he should be so honoured in a foreign court. There is something quite disarming about it, or at least it should be disarming for those writers who make much of so-called Jewish exclusivist attitudes in postexilic times. Friction occurred only at the point where the faith of Judaism was in peril. It is at that point that the urge for survival may dictate a course of behaviour not otherwise pursued.

The dream is both long and complex. Its central feature is a tree of such magnitude that it touches the sky and spreads from one end of the earth to the other. The tree often lends itself to metaphorical usage in the Hebrew Scriptures. Psalm 1 likens the person whose 'delight is in the Torah of the LORD' to 'a tree planted by streams of water . . .'. Similarly, Jeremiah compares the one 'whose trust is the LORD . . .' to 'a tree planted by water, that sends out its roots by the stream' (Jer. 17:7-8). Under this metaphor Daniel 4 speaks specifically of a kingdom, as is quite clear from v. 22. If the author was in need of a source to inspire this association, he had one ready to hand in Ezek. 31:2-18 where the exilic prophet likens the Egyptian pharaoh to:

> . . . a cedar in Lebanon,
> with fair branches and forest shade,
>   and of great height,
>   its top among the clouds.

This passage has a twofold usefulness for the author of Daniel. It promotes the image of the majestic tree but it also provides the instruction which ch. 4 is designed to demonstrate, i.e., that 'Pride goes before destruction, and a haughty spirit before a fall' (Prov. 16:18). Similar biblical material, though not as applicable as the above, may be found in Ezek. 17:22-24.

The next stage in Nebuchadnezzar's dream is reached with the appearance of 'a watcher, a holy one', who has descended from heaven (v. 13). Both Rashi and Ibn Ezra understood the first of the two underlying Aramaic words to suggest the sense of being alert, and this, coupled with the second word, led them to identify the watcher as an 'angel'. Unless we wish to postulate the existence of some other intermediary biblical being we should simply agree with these two medieval Jewish commentators. La-cocque's rendering, 'a Watcher, a Saint', is less than helpful, if not misleading, and his argument in support of 'Saint' in this context is not convincing (*Daniel*, 78-79).

The angelology of the book of Daniel, with its easy movement between heaven and earth, is further evidence of the late date of the final composition of the book.

The effectiveness of the angelic command seems to lie in the words themselves. The utterance of these words is tantamount to their execution. This is a concept not foreign to the thought of the OT. The tree is cut down, the branches lopped, the leaves strewn, the fruit scattered, and sheltering birds and beasts forced to flee. Everything happens with such suddenness that the normal processes of withering and dying are precluded. Yet it is not a complete and utter destruction. A stump is left in the ground. When the notion of incomplete destruction is found elsewhere in Scripture, it is applied to the house of David. Jeremiah preaches of the day when the scattered flock will be gathered, when God 'will raise up for David a righteous Branch [who] shall reign as king and deal wisely . . .' (Jer. 23:5). Two famous passages in Isaiah speak of 'the stump' that will remain standing (Isa. 6:13 and 11:1).

In the middle of v. 15 there is a necessary movement from the inanimate to the personal, from 'it' to 'he'. 'Let *him* be wet with the dew of heaven; let *his* lot be. . .'. The Aramaic text would allow either 'it' or 'him/he', but the plain sense of the statement, together with the interpretation in v. 25, supports the RSV translation. The metamorphosis is required at this point and not later.

Now the reason for Nebuchadnezzar's fear and alarm becomes apparent. Though there is no reason why the dream must necessarily be taken as referring to the dreamer himself, its substance alone was such as to engender in the king the reaction ascribed to him. Following fast on the destruction of the immense and majestic tree comes the chilling depiction of a man whose mind is no longer the mind of a man but that of a beast.

The translation 'mind' is to be preferred to 'heart' (Lacocque). It is not disputed, however, that the underlying Aramaic (and Hebrew) word may have a wider connotation that allows that possibility.

The duration of this rather bizarre metamorphosis is vaguely stated as 'seven times' (RSV) or 'seven periods'. The repetition of the expression in v. 23 and its interpretation in vv. 25 and 32 offer nothing more definite. No strong argument may be advanced for rendering it 'seven years', though this did appeal to both Rashi and Ibn Ezra and, in more recent times, to Hartman. Perhaps the stated period of punishment is best left in an indefinite form. The element of deliberate vagueness may serve to remove any hint of predetermination and allow us to take more seriously the conditional nature of the punishment as expressed in v. 27.

The description of the dream concludes in v. 17 with a statement which places on it the full imprimatur of God. 'The sentence is by the decree of the watchers, the decision by the word of the holy ones' (v. 17a). Not two separate groups of divine messengers are referred to here but only one. The recent Stuttgart edition of the Masoretic Text (BHS) puts vv. 10b-17a (7b-14a in Hebrew) in metric form, thus making more obvious the presence in v. 17a of the poetic device known as synonymous parallelism. An expression receives emphasis by means of its repetition. No matter how important their function, the angels are no more than the emissaries of God. They exist to carry out his will and, in this case, to proclaim his absolute sovereignty. In the prophetic literature the prophets themselves serve a similar purpose. As members of the 'council' of God they make known his 'counsel'. In this matter the angels do not usurp the role of the prophets, for this inner council of God is portrayed as existing during the prophetic period (see Job 1:6-12). With the demise of prophecy, for whatever reason, and the increasing frequency of apocalyptic literary expression, however, the angels assume an importance not hitherto required. The presence of these intermediaries becomes more immediate.

With v. 17b we come to the heart of the message of this chapter. The recipient of the punishment is to be brought to know that 'the Most High rules the kingdom of men, and gives it to whom he wills, and sets over it the lowliest of men'. In a form omitting the last clause these words occur again in vv. 25 and 32, and the same central point is made in vv. 26 and 35. This is the lesson to be learned by Nebuchadnezzar, and it is to be brought home to him in a devastatingly personal way. But it is a lesson that is here given the widest possible reference: 'that the living may know . . .'; 'that all who live may learn' (Hartman). The king is thus made to serve the purpose of the storyteller, whose chief audience is his compatriots.

This section closes with Nebuchadnezzar's repetition of his confidence in Daniel, who in fact is the king's last hope. All others have proved unhelpful, quite unequal to the task.

19-27 Understandably, Daniel is hesitant and requires the assurance of Nebuchadnezzar before he is willing to proceed with what he well knows to be a most unpalatable interpretation. Even then he prefaces his remarks with the plea that what he has to say will not result in any misfortune to the king but in injury to his enemies. The first part of the dream is repeated word for word (vv. 20-21); then follows the interpretation. The tree is the king. Step by step Nebuchadnezzar has his dream recapitulated and its interpretation spelled out. The full measure of his misfortune is recited: he will be 'driven from among men'; he will dwell 'with the beasts of the field', and so on. But then the first important qualification is introduced (the second is in v. 27). It is not a limitless punishment. It will have served its purpose when he comes to acknowledge the sovereignty of the Most High (v. 25). The stump is the guarantee of the eventual continuation of his kingdom. What has happened is that Nebuchadnezzar has been taken at his word. The expressions of faith attributed to him in 3:28-29, and more particularly in 2:47, now come home to him with a force with which he had not reckoned.

The question of the relatedness of one chapter to another in the first part of the book of Daniel is not an easy one. As stated earlier it is improper to impose on this material the burden of detailed correspondence. Yet it would be invalid to postulate the presence and contribution of a compiler/author without having recognised certain signs of unity. This is not to speak in terms of an overall unity within these chapters, much less the book as a whole, but it is to take seriously the extant book as the work of someone who had a clear notion of the central message he wished to convey. Many scholars have pointed to signs of independent origin of some of the early chapters. The book, in its present form, also shows unmistakable signs of a theological and religious purposefulness. The compiler, in good Hebraic fashion, has not removed all the 'rough spots', but he has dexterously woven his material to serve his main aim. This may be one reason why Nebuchadnezzar appears in ch. 4 when the initial subject may have been Nabonidus (see below under v. 33).

Verse 25 speaks of the sovereignty of God, the necessary corollary of which is his freedom. He gives the kingdom 'to whom he will'. This is by no means a novel assertion. The author would have to do no more than reflect on the beginning of God's relationship with Israel to find ample corroboration. This special bond depended on nothing that was inherently a part of Israel but solely on the action of God (see Deut. 9:4-6). If further proof were needed it could be found in the prophet Amos's stern warning in 9:7.

The use of the term 'Heaven' for the deity (v. 26) is not found elsewhere in the OT. Montgomery comments: 'For the first time in Jewish religion we meet with "Heaven" as surrogate for "God" ' (*Daniel*, 239). It is found in later Jewish writings (1 Macc. 3:19; 4:10, 40) to avoid the use of the word 'God'. Lacocque's rendering, 'the heavens', reads most oddly, and what linguistic support there is for it may be more apposite in another context.

The dream has been restated, the interpretation given, and the judgment pronounced, but it is not absolute. The author introduces an element of the conditional, a persistent feature of earlier prophetic preaching. It is not a condition that will allow full absolution, but it 'may perhaps' (v. 27) bring about some amelioration. The terms are interesting. 'Break off [discontinue] your sins by practising righteousness, and your iniquities by showing mercy to the oppressed.' The RSV translation can be improved on. The Hebrew (Aramaic) word underlying 'righteousness' may be better rendered 'good deeds'. Very seldom in the OT is the word 'righteousness' a satisfactory rendering, but it would appear to have become a habit with most translators. 'The oppressed' or, better, 'the weak', refers to those members of society who cannot fend for themselves, those who are vulnerable. The concern expressed in this verse is found throughout the Pentateuch and the prophetic literature.

Hartman's translation, 'atone for your sins', has neither textual nor contextual warrant. From time to time attempts have been made to read into this verse more than is present. It cannot be stressed too strongly that it shows no trace of any Jewish doctrine of salvation. Neither in the Hebrew Scriptures nor in later Jewish religious thought is there the statement that one's salvation is dependent on what one is able to achieve. Jewish faith is no less subject to the grace of God than is the Christian faith. Where misunderstanding creeps in is in the persistent practice of attempting to define the former in terms that are appropriate only to the latter. Though they have much in common, not least the Hebrew Scriptures, the two faiths have quite disparate language by which they seek to describe their relationship to God.

The advice given to Nebuchadnezzar in v. 27 is that he should 'mend his ways'. Then, and only then, may there perhaps be a lengthening of his tranquility, i.e., a return to and continuation of the pleasant state described in v. 4 of this chapter.

28-33 These verses are in the third person in contradistinction to vv. 4-27 and 34-37, which are in the first. They are meant to describe the events that immediately led up to the fulfilment of the interpretation as well as the fulfilment itself. Our reading of chs. 2 and 3 might have led us to expect some exchange of words between Nebuchadnezzar and Daniel at this point. However, that is not to be. The latter now moves out of the story, and Nebuchadnezzar's response must await the conclusion of his period of chastisement.

Verse 28 anticipates the outcome. Presumably Daniel's counsel in v. 27 went unheeded. There was no change for the better in Nebuchadnezzar's behaviour, nor as yet any change in his estate. Twelve months after the events just described he was 'taking the air' on the roof of his palace surveying the wonders of the city of Babylon, more or less his own creation, thinking perhaps that the dream would never catch up with him. Then, at the very moment when he was so overwhelmed by pride in his own achievement, a voice 'fell . . . from heaven' (v. 31). The sentence is pronounced as swiftly as Nathan's accusatory word to King David: 'You are the man!' (2 Sam. 12:7). Neither king had a chance to deflect the word of judgment. For Nebuchadnezzar, so the story continues, it entailed all that Daniel had predicted, loss of kingdom and human company, loss also of the faculty that had been used to build a great city and to govern a great empire.

Does this have any historical basis? Are there any records suggesting that what is described in v. 33 did befall Nebuchadnezzar? If a negative reply is given to these questions, it is not wholly on the grounds of an argument from silence. Nebuchadnezzar was an extremely important king; his reign extended a little over four decades from 605 to 562 B.C.E. and was well documented. Nothing would indicate an absence from regal duties nor give any evidence of abnormal behaviour.

Scholars have long entertained the possibility that the monarch whose insanity is described in ch. 4 was not Nebuchadnezzar but the last of the neo-Babylonian rulers, Nabonidus (Nabunaid), whose reign spanned the period from 556 to 539 B.C.E. For part of this time he was absent from Babylon, preferring to spend his time in Teima in Arabia, an area that he had previously conquered, and where he pursued the study of astrology. This information is available from what is known as the 'Nabonidus Chronicle', published in 1882 (J. B. Pritchard, ed., *Ancient Near Eastern Texts relating to the OT*, 305-7). Nabonidus was something of a heretic by Babylonian religious standards. He failed to give due deference to the god Marduk, the head of the Babylonian pantheon, thereby incurring the wrath of the priests. An account of their diatribe against the king is to be found in another ancient document, 'Nabonidus and the Clergy of Babylon' (*ANET*, 312-15). While this does not contain the accusation that he was insane, there is sufficient polemical matter of a derogatory nature to have him popularly regarded as a man of highly unusual, if not eccentric, behaviour.

Among the important finds at Qumran is a writing referred to as 'The Prayer of Nabonidus' (4Q Prayer of Nabonidus). The text contains a number of lacunae but enough survives to give a description of how, for seven years, Nabonidus suffered in Teima from 'a bad inflammation' (or 'bad ulcer'). He was cured of this malady by a Jewish exorcist who pardoned his sins and induced him to give glory to the Most High God. The differences between this experience and that of Nebuchadnezzar in ch. 4 should not be overlooked. There is sufficient general likeness, however, to keep the issue of identification alive. The whole matter becomes all the more intriguing when we recall that Daniel 5 refers to Belshazzar, who virtually took over the throne if not the title of king during the absence of his father Nabonidus, as the son of Nebuchadnezzar (5:2, 11, 13, 18). The shift from Nebuchadnezzar to Nabonidus is likely to have been quite deliberate on the part of the author. The one around whom the story was fashioned was a great king, a monarch with an illustrious name. The other was by comparison a nonentity. If we were concerned in these stories with accurate historical recollection we might have cause to ponder a significant difficulty. But, as the purpose of the storyteller is quite other than that, we can afford to allow our natural propensity for critical analysis to be suspended as we listen to what the text has to say.

It is to be noted that the Qumran discoveries include not only a number of fragments from three separate caves comprising in all a sizeable section of the canonical book of Daniel but a quantity of related material as well. Hengel advances the suggestion that the keen interest in this type of material within the community of Qumran, one of the two major successors to the Hasidim, may indicate that 'we are dealing not just with one book, but, as in the case of Enoch, with a whole cycle, probably backed by a school' (*Judaism and Hellenism*, 1:176). The 'Prayer of Nabonidus', preserved by this group, points to an earlier form of the ch. 4 story.

34-37 We are not told how long Nebuchadnezzar's disability lasted. The phrase 'at the end of the days' is as indefinite as is 'seven times'. Animal behaviour now gives place to human, and his first action, the raising of his eyes heavenward, illustrates with singular effect the great difference between the two. Only mankind is said to have been made in the image of God (Gen. 1:26-27). The return of 'reason' is also meant to signify this regaining of his birthright. The next action is as logical for the biblical writer as those that have preceded it. Nebuchadnezzar, again truly human and thoroughly chastened, offers to the Most High both praise and honour in words that recall the opening doxology. They appear in like form in 6:26 and 7:14, 27 and, beyond the book of Daniel, in Ps. 145:13.

Nebuchadnezzar is finally brought to the point where he both recognises and extols the sovereignty of God. The will of God is current not only among the 'host of heaven', the angelic beings that are at all times responsive to his commands, but among the 'inhabitants of earth' as well. There is no questioning of the rightness or wrongness of what has happened to him. God has demonstrated to him that 'all his words are right and his ways are just; and those who walk in pride he is able to abase' (v. 37). See also Ps. 111:7. In this happy state his thoughts are far removed from the age-old problem of theodicy. Jeremiah, Habakkuk, and Job are for the moment silenced (cf. Jer. 12:1; Hab. 1:2-4; Job 9:2; 10:4-7; 23). If, however, the author had in mind not Nebuchadnezzar and his misuse of power, but Antiochus Epiphanes and his oppression of the faithful, what else could he preach but a message that put the case for justice in the boldest terms and yet contained an unequivocal word of hope? In the light of what he has yet to say in 12:1-3 any criticism begins to pale.

In closing the comments on this chapter, we note that the title given to God, 'the King of heaven', is not found elsewhere in the Scriptures. It is similar to the expression used in 5:23 and also occurs in 1 Esdr. 4:46ff. Its use here is a further sign of the late composition of the book as it now stands.

CHAPTER 5

THE WRITING ON THE WALL
Daniel 5:1-31

The two chief figures in this story are Daniel and Belshazzar. The latter appears for the first time, and the description of him as 'king' and as the son of Nebuchadnezzar has occasioned some difficulty and not a little discussion. These matters will be taken up in the course of the commentary, but for the moment we note some points of contact between this story and the preceding one.

The most obvious link is the one to which reference has already been made, the portrayal of Belshazzar as the son of Nebuchadnezzar. This allows the author to weave his plot around the theme that was central to ch. 4, namely, that arrogance leads to a fall. In this case it is the fall not merely of the man but of the empire. The example of Nebuchadnezzar and his eventual display of humility are made to stand in the starkest contrast with the unabashed pride of Belshazzar. So closely are these two stories related that in 5:18-21 there is an almost word for word borrowing from the previous chapter. Though the relationship of the one king to the other may be open to question, for the purposes of the author it is not only significant but central. The description of Daniel as one in whom there is 'the spirit of the holy gods' (4:9; 5:11, 14) is a further though less pivotal common feature.

It is possible that a story such as is found in ch. 5 had independent currency within the Babylonian diaspora. If so, the form in which it circulated would most likely have been independent of ch. 4 and much less complex than it is in its extant state. What we have before us in the text of these two chapters comes from a late hand. It was of little consequence to the author that to heighten the drama and underline the message he had to move beyond the restrictions of historically accurate detail. Had he been aware of all the trouble he was to cause by doing this he might have been tempted to add a few footnotes!

1-4 'King Belshazzar made a great feast. . . .' The historicity of Belshazzar is not an issue. That there was such a ruler (the exact rendering of the Aramaic word is not important), who was in a position to be depicted in a like historical setting, is attested independently of Scripture. That much is beyond debate. The historicity of the *story*, however, is quite another matter, because on this hinges our understanding of what the OT is or is not. There is a sense in which the two words 'historicity' and 'story' are so disparate in connotation that they do not belong together. If 'historicity' is posited only of those records which by their nature and purpose should be an accurate record of what actually happened, then it is doubtful whether anything in the OT, beyond the most mundane, could ever be so described. Most of the so-called historical narratives of the Scriptures would be excluded from such description. On the other hand, if the term 'historicity' may be applied to something that is related to the experience of a people, that could not have arisen but for that experience, and that continues to be related to the ongoing life of that people, then much of the OT otherwise excluded is encompassed by it. To varying degrees the stories of the first half of the book of Daniel come within that range. If by 'story' is meant 'fiction', then some other word should be found. If, however, a more sensible approach is adopted, and by 'story' is meant the substance of a 'telling' or of a 'recital', there is no reason why we cannot speak of the *historicity* of a story. Only on the grounds of a narrow and erroneous understanding of either of these terms are they reckoned to be mutually exclusive. It is necessary to use the words 'story' and 'storyteller' when dealing with the material of Daniel 1 – 6, but it is also necessary to assert its essential historicity.

Efforts to 'iron out' the inaccuracies in the stories, say in the description of Belshazzar as the son of Nebuchadnezzar (5:22), betray signs of an uneasiness which logically may not be removed until every inaccuracy is dealt with and every difficulty resolved. This unease leads to forced and unnatural argumentation. Without question Belshazzar was not the son of Nebuchadnezzar but of Nabonidus. To assert that here the word 'son' may be taken as 'grandson' or in some other extended sense, despite the fact that this is semantically possible, is to fail to come to terms with the point of the story. Belshazzar is condemned precisely because the example he might have followed was so close to him that it removed all possible excuse. The word 'father' is used of Nebuchadnezzar's relationship to Belshazzar in vv. 2, 11, 13, and 18. If we recall the strong possibility that the subject of madness in ch. 4 is Nabonidus and not Nebuchadnezzar, we can readily understand the reason for the shift in ch. 5. It is Nebuchadnezzar, the great king and conqueror of Judah, who is made to displace the rather pitiable and relatively insignificant Nabonidus.

Does not the importance of ch. 5 lie, not in the absolute accuracy of details concerning persons and relationships, but in the fact that there is a king of Babylon who had before him the example of his father's divine chastisement and eventual humility, but who chose, not only to neglect that example, but to act in open defiance of the God of Israel by desecrating the sacred Jerusalem temple vessels? It is not in the strict verification of the details that we hear the word, but in listening to what is being said.

The great feast of King Belshazzar was not over-large by oriental regal standards, though its fateful timing afforded it a passage into history not given the usual celebration of this kind. There was a tradition current in the ancient world, mentioned by both Herodotus and Xenophon, that while the king was engaged in banqueting the combined armies of the Medes and Persians launched a surprise attack on Babylon. In the book of Esther we read of a feast given by the Persian monarch Ahasuerus for his princes and officials that lasted for 180 days (Esth. 1:1-8). Unlike the celebration recorded in Daniel 5, the main gathering excluded women. Queen Vashti there presided over a separate function (1:9).

Verse 1 serves to set the scene. The drama begins with v. 2. Both Rashi and Ibn Ezra would have Belshazzar acting under the influence of wine. This rendering is also followed by S. R. Driver and more recently by Hartman. The RSV's 'when he tasted wine' chooses not to interpret. Whatever the state of Belshazzar at the time, what followed was, in the storyteller's judgment, a rash and perverse act for which his downfall and death could be the only just outcome. That some of the sacred temple vessels were brought to Babylon is mentioned at the very beginning of the book (1:2) and attested in 2 Kgs. 24:10-13, though the latter source gives a somewhat more complex account (cf. 2 Kgs. 25:13-16 and 2 Chr. 36:18). After the proclamation of Cyrus's edict permitting the exiled Jews to return to their home state, Sheshbazzar was given custody of the vessels, which according to Ezra 1:10 included 'thirty bowls of gold, two thousand four hundred and ten bowls of silver'. If this were so, then each of Belshazzar's guests, his thousand lords plus his wives and concubines, had no difficulty in acquiring a handsome vessel with which to continue the bacchanalian festivity. Not content merely to demonstrate what seemed to him to be a better use for foreign sacred cups, however, Belshazzar, encouraged now no doubt by the enthusiasm of the gathering, overstepped the mark completely. He began to use them in his praise of 'the gods of gold and silver, bronze, iron, wood, and stone' (v. 4). It was this deliberate act of gross sacrilege that was to bring down on him the wrath of Daniel's God. At least that was the immediate cause. The reader of the book of Daniel in the 2nd cent. B.C.E. and in the 20th cent. C.E. is instructed by it to expect the fall of every kingdom with one exception and one alone. Belshazzar's blind stupidity hastened an inevitable end. There is no direct parallel between the Babylonian king's action in 539 B.C.E. and that of the Seleucid monarch's defiling of the temple in 167 B.C.E., but it was of the same general order and, as such, invited comparison. The early story, perhaps from the 4th or 3rd cent. B.C.E., was to lose none of its original force and, like those of its collection, was to take on a new and added significance when Daniel's people were pressed in a way not hitherto experienced.

5-9 It is not at all clear that Lacocque (*Daniel*, 93 and 95) is correct when he asserts that the king alone saw the vision, though his interpretative comment on that point is thought-provoking. Certainly the text mentions only the king, for after all, at this stage of the story, he is the most important character. It could be that the express mention of the location of the 'lampstand' is to suggest that the hand and the writing were visible to all. Of course there could be no doubt that the strange event was related to the king. It was scarcely possible for some lesser being now to become the focus of attention and so upstage the king himself.

Verse 6 provides us with an almost amusingly graphic picture of a man suddenly overcome with terror. He grew pale, he became bewildered (RSV 'his thoughts alarmed him'), his legs gave way, and his knees knocked. It is not without its humourous touch. We have a similar description of physical and mental collapse in Nah. 2:10 in the prophet's description of what will be the reaction of the hated Nineveh when its day of judgment comes. The opening verse of that book might well have served as a text for Daniel 5:

The LORD is a jealous God and avenging,
  the LORD is avenging and wrathful.
The LORD takes vengeance on his adversaries,
  and keeps wrath for his enemies. (Nah. 1:2)

First Nineveh, then Babylon. As in two of the previous stories (chs. 2 and 4), the monarch is able to fall back on the professional interpreters who seemingly are forever standing ready for just such an occasion as this. One is tempted to see in them the ancient world's equivalent of modern television's analyst. The story itself does not depart from the expected pattern. Great rewards are offered but the local Chaldeans and astrologers fail dismally. It would be no exaggeration to claim that the reader knows that this will happen. There is a pattern in the Daniel stories which enables one to anticipate the outcome at almost every point. Nor will the reader (or hearer) be any less interested, or in any way less enthusiastic, for having read (or heard) the same story over and over again. The purpose of such stories is that they should be treated in this way. It is their genius that they lose nothing in this constant retelling.

In intent and in effect, though not in form, this method of communication is not unlike that of the Indonesian (Malayan) 'wayang', which is primarily a morality play in which the forces of good triumph over the forces of evil. Those who attend the 'wayang' performance know the plot from beginning to end and, except for the occasional topical insertion, able to follow each line of the play word for word. The whole theatre, not just the stage, is where the play is being acted out. But this in no way detracts from the excitement of the moment, nor from the sense of relief and satisfaction when the curtain falls. The end may be anticipated, but it is always received with a freshness and a zeal

as though this were its first occurrence. And for all the telling
and retelling the outcome of each play is no less welcome, for it
has accomplished what it set out to do. The ordinary citizen,
otherwise forgotten, and so often encircled by those same forces
of evil, finds in the display of right's ultimate victory some hope
that his or her life may take a similar course. The points where
the 'wayang' ceases to be parallel to the Daniel story are obvious.
Not least of these is the peculiarly theological dimension in the
latter. But the similarities are strong for the simple reason that
such appeal to human sentiment moves beyond cultural and ethnic boundaries. It is universal. The 'wayang' has a role in Indonesian life similar to that played by canonical Scripture. In
any consideration of the reasons for the eventual 'canonisation'
of the book of Daniel, it would be unwise to rule out the importance of popular appeal.

The task set the wise men was twofold. It was necessary to
read the writing, and then to interpret it (v. 7). Despite their
collective talents they were unable to meet the demands even of
the first test. We can only conjecture the reason for this failure.
Either the words were written in an unknown script, or they were
presented in such a way that it was not possible to make sense
of them. Given this lack of clarity in the story itself, it is not
surprising that commentators down through the ages have offered a spate of possible reasons for the difficulty encountered by
the wise men.

Later Jewish commentators suggested a cryptic rearrangement
of the letters, e.g., by having the words stand in a vertical rather
than a horizontal form, or by the transposition of certain letters.
Fascinating as these proffered solutions are, they probably ex-
aggerate the difficulty. It is unlikely that we need to posit a
strange script or a cryptic order of letters to account for the
dilemma of the wise men.

The rewards for the successful candidate were considerable
(v. 7). Mordecai was rewarded for his service to the Persian king
some two or three generations later than the supposed setting of
ch. 5 by being allowed to wear 'royal robes of blue and white
. . . and a mantle of fine linen and purple' (Esth. 8:15). Joseph,
another Hebrew hero who was to rise to great heights in a foreign
court, received from the Egyptian pharaoh 'garments of fine linen,
and . . . a gold chain about his neck' (Gen. 41:42). These were

the outward signs of an office the status of which was to be 'the
third ruler in the kingdom' (v. 7). The RSV rendering, which is
borne out by 6:1-3, is to be preferred to the alternative '[he] shall
rule one third of the kingdom' (Rashi, Ibn Ezra). Handsome
though the rewards were, they proved to be beyond the grasp of
the Babylonian rivals. With their failure the king's consternation
grew; his complexion became more ashen, and, as might well be
expected, his honored guests began to exhibit real signs of agi-
tation (v. 9).

10-12   An interesting feature of two of the Daniel stories (chs. 2
and 5) is the need for the hero to be introduced to the monarch
when no such introduction would appear to be required. This is
probably no more than a literary device, but it is an effective
one. The calling in of the unknown hero, though of course anything but unknown to the reader, and his success, where the
readily available professionals have failed, add lustre to the cause
being championed by the author. On this occasion the one who
acts as entrepreneur is, according to the RSV, 'the queen', but
it is most likely that we are to understand by the Aramaic word,
'the queen mother'. The important role that she plays and the
manner of her entry would suggest that some such figure is intended, and not merely the wife of the reigning king for whom
behaviour of this type would be out of keeping with ancient Near
Eastern protocol. We are given a glimpse of queen-motherly as-
pirations in the machinations of Bathsheba (1 Kings 1), while
the powerful nature of the office can be seen in Athaliah's actions
described in 2 Kgs. 11:1-3. In Daniel 5 the senior royal lady is
mother of Belshazzar and widow of Nebuchadnezzar.

The regent is reminded that there is in the realm a man whose
prowess in matters of dream and vision interpretation has been
well attested. The description of Daniel in vv. 11 and 12 far surpasses anything encountered hitherto. Not only does he possess
the 'spirit of the holy gods' (4:8, 9, 18), but his wisdom can be
compared to that of the gods themselves (v. 11). Moreover, his
power to interpret dreams is only one of a number of singular
accomplishments. He is able to 'explain riddles' and to 'solve
problems'. What is meant precisely by these latter feats is not at
all clear, but they indicate that Daniel is the type of practitioner
who stands firmly in the ancient tradition of the wise man. He

also has about him something of the seer (see 1 Samuel 9). What he is now called upon to undertake will require a combination of these esoteric gifts.

With Belshazzar in a stricken and befuddled state it is necessary for his mother to take over the proceedings. Her advice in v. 12, 'Now let Daniel be called', borders on an authoritative command.

13-16 Despite the deliberate links with other chapters, and with ch. 4 in particular, there is a fair measure of independence in this story as in each of the others. The striving for effective storytelling, together with some degree of continuity, produces the occasional hiatus which no amount of 20th-cent. Western ingenuity is able to remove. Here in ch. 5 the man Daniel appears with all his previously earned credentials and with the associations which have helped to mold him as a heroic figure, but these are not allowed to hinder a new rise to fame. For the moment, in this new story and fresh situation, it is not Daniel the chief magician whom the reader meets but Daniel the Jew, the hero of his people. In a sense he is a lonely figure, as lonely as any of his reader compatriots; and the power he has comes, not from any office he might hold, but from the God of every Jew. In reading the stories of Daniel the issue is not what makes sense when one story is compared with another but what was the required form of the story if it was to have its desired effect on the intended audience. Of primary importance in the interpretation of biblical material of this type is the far from simple task of attempting to understand the rapport between hero and reader. If this attempt is made, the modern reader is at least more likely to move beyond the temptation to approach this literature as though it were in the area of historiography. As an illustration of the dampening effect of a historiographical approach it is simply noted that if the chronology of the book is taken seriously our hero is now a man of advanced years, having been in exile almost seven decades. The Daniel of the stories, however, does not age!

The king's description of what has occurred lacks all sense of urgency; nor does this clearly stated summary of events reveal any indication of his state of advanced anxiety and physical disarray (vv. 6, 9). Rather hurriedly the author has Daniel introduced and brought up to date with what has happened. To have expanded at this point would have led to a diminishing of the tension.

17-30 Almost peremptorily Daniel waves aside the proffered rewards, but he does agree to read the writing and give its interpretation. There is probably an intended lesson in this for the author's compatriots. It is essential for the embellishment of the figure of Daniel that he should be the recipient of high rewards and that he should gain a position of eminence within the state. Nothing in his religion declared that he should refuse. In this, too, he was an object lesson. But it was also necessary to point to his selflessness here and elsewhere. What he has received in the past has followed as a consequence of services given. He has not set out to advance himself. Self-deprecation is contrary to the rules of faith; so, too, is self-seeking. Service is its own reward, and those who serve faithfully to the end receive the promise of resurrection (12:1-3).

The high calling of Daniel is no more clearly expressed than in the lecture he delivers to the powerful Belshazzar. The king will most certainly receive an answer to the enigmatic writing on the wall but not without a prefacing word of censure and condemnation. Nowhere in the book does Daniel come as close to the classical prophets as he does in vv. 18-23. The confrontation with Belshazzar is worthy of an Amos or a Jeremiah. The author, who has already seen the hand of God behind the siege and sacking of Jerusalem (1:2), has no difficulty in ascribing to God himself the greatness and glory of Nebuchadnezzar. If there is a theological difficulty here, it is no greater than can be found elsewhere in Scripture (see under ch. 1). The mandate God gave Nebuchadnezzar is as wide-sweeping as that of any monarch mentioned in the OT. It extends even to the power of life and death (v. 19). As a description of the behaviour of an oriental despot, this is in keeping with known practices. Perhaps the issue of the divine sanctioning of Nebuchadnezzar's deeds should not be pressed too far. The lesson that the author would have Daniel draw for the edification of Belshazzar, a lesson based on the example of his 'father', can best be made by the use of dramatic imagery. It is necessary for Nebuchadnezzar to be depicted as 'larger than life' if the ensuing prophetic words are to have the desired effect. The arrogant exercise of power and the boastful flaunting of achievement, this deliberate overstepping of the divinely ordained limit, must result in the collapse of the kingdom and the punishment of the man (vv. 20-21).

As pride had led to Nebuchadnezzar's downfall, so the act of humility had resulted in his restoration. Were Belshazzar to apply to himself the implications of this divine lesson he would remain secure. Yet, not content merely to disregard what the past had to teach, he took the battle to God himself. In doing so he failed to realise that the tokens of Israel's defeat, the captured sacred objects of the God of Israel, were in fact the sure signs of God's victory. Israel had gone into captivity not because of the weakness of its God but because of his strength. The seemingly victorious gods whom Belshazzar now praised were totally unable to come to his aid. They were no more than they appeared to be, gold, silver, wood, and stone (v. 23). What he had failed to recognise was that ultimately he was answerable not to them but to the God of history and creation, in whose very power was his life's breath (Gen. 2:7). His sin was not so much the desecration of the sacred temple vessels as the blasphemous spurning of the universal God.

The great anonymous prophet of the Exile, Deutero-Isaiah, had made this point time and time again. Since his day there could be no question in the mind of any Jewish author that there was one God and one God only to whom not just he but the whole of mankind was responsible. This appreciation of the universal sovereignty of the God who had made himself known in the Exodus and at Mt. Sinai, who had led his often recalcitrant people not just through one wilderness but through many, was the touchstone of postexilic faith and understanding. For the author of Daniel the writing on the wall could have one Source and one alone.

Just four words were inscribed on the wall: *Mene, Mene, Tekel, Parsin* (with the conjunction written *Upharsin*; v. 25). The interpretation follows immediately (vv. 26-28), but it is not related directly or with absolute accuracy to all four words. From the interpretation given it would appear that the duplication of the first word is not integral to the message, and the meaning of the final word is attained by reading a singular form and not the plural or dual form of the original. This interpretative reduction to three words with the use of the singular form, *Peres*, corre-

sponds to the form of the original inscription given in the Septuagint, Theodotion, the Vulgate, and Josephus. This is rather
weighty evidence in favour of a simpler reading in v. 25. Though
it brings the original inscription into line with its interpretation,
it does not explain how the more complex and more difficult form
is to be found in v. 25 of the MT as it stands. Two initial possibilities present themselves:

(i) there is no real disparity between the inscription and its
interpretation once it is realised that any interpretation has
an acceptable latitude;

(ii) the words of the inscription contain a meaning over
and above that given in the stated interpretation.

The first argument is a neat and simple solution and precludes
further speculation. The second allows for the possibility that
those for whom the story was meant would be able to see below
the surface to a deeper and more significant meaning. After all,
the interpretation given is only a slightly less than accurate description of what did happen in the year 539 B.C.E. (the date of
Cyrus's capture of Babylon and of Belshazzar's death). When it
is recalled that the script in which the earliest readers would have
received the text allowed verbal variation by the insertion of
different collections of vowels, the argument for some kind of
esoteric meaning receives considerable support. The difficulty, of
course, lies in finding the clues. Almost a century ago, Clermont-
Ganneau advanced the thesis that the terms are measurements
of weight, namely, mina, tekel (the Aramaic equivalent of shekel),
and peres. By this means the motif of successive kingdoms already encountered in ch. 2, and which features so prominently
in the second half of the book, could be applied to the inscription,
albeit in a modified form. The subjects could be the last kings of
the neo-Babylonian regime. It must be admitted that all this is
in the area of speculation. Fuller treatment is given in the commentaries of Hartman and Lacocque. When we turn to the explanation in vv. 26-28 we are at least on firm ground.

Throughout the interpretation the author has Daniel engage
in paronomasia, a frequently used verbal device in the prophetic
literature (e.g., Amos 8:1, 2 and Jer. 1:11, 12). The ominous
expression 'your days are numbered' has crept into common
usage in the English language. Presumably it owes its origin to

Dan. 5:26, though the notion of keeping a tally of one's days is to be found in Ps. 90:12. There the outcome is beneficial, whereas the divine numbering in Daniel spells doom. A further word-play has Belshazzar 'weighed in the balances and found wanting', and finally a double play on the word *Peres* presages both the division of the kingdom and its parceling out to the Persians and the Medes.

It is less than helpful to speculate on what effect this message may have had on Belshazzar. The storyteller moves away from the villain to the hero. The former's task is simply to make the promised rewards to a reluctant Daniel, or at least that is what is suggested by v. 17.

The end comes swiftly (v. 30). Belshazzar is denied time even to contemplate the ill-fated message. With his overthrow, or rather with the surrender of the city, the neo-Babylonian empire moved over to make way for another. In its time it had conquered Assyria, confined Egypt to its own territory, and overrun many lesser states including Judah. But true to the message of the book of Daniel, time runs out for every empire of human creation. Babylon was no exception. The thrust of the prophet Jeremiah's prophecy was borne out, not word for word, but in its general and overall effect:

> 'Behold, I am against you, O proud one,
>   says the Lord GOD of hosts;
> for your day has come,
>   the time when I will punish you.
> The proud one shall stumble and fall,
>   with none to raise him up,
> and I will kindle a fire in his cities,
>   and it will devour all that is round about him'.
>   (Jer. 50:31-32)

As things turned out, the city of Babylon itself fell to Cyrus (not to 'Darius the Mede') without a battle. In the Nabonidus Chronicle its capitulation is depicted in this way:

> On the 15th day, Sippar was seized without battle. Nabonidus fled. The 16th day, Gobryas (Ugbaru), the governor of Gutium, and the army of Cyrus entered Babylon without battle. Afterwards Nabonidus was arrested in Babylon when he returned (there). (*ANET*, 306)

Confirmation can be found in the laudatory Cyrus Cylinder where the relevant passage portrays the conquering Cyrus as the chosen instrument of Marduk, the chief god of the Babylonian pantheon. In this account Nabonidus is removed because of his apostasy and Babylon is taken 'without any battle' (*ANET*, 315). These contemporary accounts are to be preferred to the extremely brief reference to the same event in Dan. 5:30-31, for there the interest is in the drama, not the detail.

The final verse of ch. 5 in the MT is the introduction to the succeeding story. Although this commentary follows the chapter divisions of the RSV it has been thought proper to discuss the problem of the enigmatic 'Darius the Mede' there rather than at this point.

CHAPTER 6

THE TWO DECREES
Daniel 6:1-28

This chapter would be partly rescued from over-familiarity if it were to be entitled not 'Daniel in the Lion's Den', but 'Darius and the Two Decrees'. For that is what it is, a tale of two royal proclamations. One would have resulted in the death of Daniel but for the intervention of God. The other, promulgated by the same king, was to proclaim the worship of the God of Daniel throughout the whole realm.

In the closing verse of the previous chapter the reader is introduced to 'Darius the Mede', a figure who appears not only throughout ch. 6, but also as the reigning monarch at the time of Daniel's third vision (9:1). There is little doubt that in the author's line of kingly succession this Darius, ostensibly the conqueror of Babylon, precedes Cyrus the Great. Yet it is not possible to account for the existence of such a ruler. He receives no mention in the Chronicler's account of the events of this time either in 2 Chronicles 36 or Ezra 1. The deeds of Cyrus are recalled, but Darius makes no appearance at all (1 Chr. 36:20-23; Ezra 1:1-4). Try as some scholars might, they have not been able to show convincingly that there is a place for a 'Darius the Mede' in that period of Babylonian history between the overthrow of Nabonidus/Belshazzar (539 B.C.E.) and the accession of Cyrus II (539-530). In the opening verse of ch. 9 the Darius referred to is described as 'the son of Ahasuerus, by birth a Mede, who became king over the realm of the Chaldeans' (9:1). In this context 'Chaldeans' is used in its ethnic sense and is to be equated with 'Babylonians'.

In the book of Esther a King Ahasuerus appears as the Persian monarch who befriends Mordecai and takes Esther as his wife. This monarch is presumably Xerxes I (486-465), himself the son of Darius I Hystaspes (522-486), the Persian ruler defeated at the Battle of Marathon in 490 B.C.E. Most likely it is this latter king who, for reasons mentioned below, lent his personage and his title to the Daniel 6 story. There is no trace of a Darius contemporary with Cyrus the Great, and the depiction of such a ruler as son-in-law of Cyrus (*Yosippon* iii), or his kinsman (Josephus, *Ant.* x.11.4), is no more than an attempt to find some feasible solution to an early and persistent difficulty.

The last king of the Median empire was Astyages, whose rule came to an end in 549 B.C.E., an early victim of the all-conquering Cyrus. It would not be beyond the bounds of possibility for Astyages to have had a descendant whose name was Darius, who may have been described as a Mede, and who could have taken part in the service of the army which entered Babylon. For a member of an already defeated and replaced royal house to be designated as conqueror of Babylon, if that is what is to be inferred from 5:31, however, would be most unlikely. Any argument to the contrary would seem to be at odds with the clear evidence contained by the Cyrus Cylinder (*ANET*, 315).

One of the concerns of the author of the book of Daniel was to show how past prophetic words had been vindicated in events that had already occurred or would be fulfilled in events yet to occur (e.g., 9:2). The dictates of his methodology would require him to take seriously the prophetic predictions concerning the affairs not only of his own people but of those nations that were caught up in God's overall plan. One such nation was Babylon. Like Assyria before it, Babylon was, in the preaching of the prophets, the chosen instrument of the divine purpose. But as with Assyria, a time would come when the conqueror itself would be conquered. Both Isaiah and Jeremiah predicted that Babylon would fall at the hands of the Medes, and there was good reason to see this as a distinct possibility (Isa. 13:17; 21:2; Jer. 51:11, 28-29). As events turned out, Media itself fell to Cyrus the Persian, and so was prevented from carrying out its prophetically predicted part in the history of the nations. That it was overrun by Persians has further coloured later reconstruction of events, for it was not uncommon in Greek and Minean accounts for the term Mede to be used loosely for Persian. An added complication is that Darius I was involved in the retaking of Babylon in 520 B.C.E. in the course of putting down an attempted coup. His penchant for organization and administration, and the association of his name with legal reform, help to form the picture of the man presented to us in the Daniel story. Moreover, the friendly attitude of Darius towards Daniel may reflect the help and encouragement given by Darius I Hystaspes to those Jews who were to be involved in the rebuilding of the Jerusalem temple (see Ezra 6:1-12, especially vv. 8-12).

This composite Darius of ch. 6, friend of the hero, organizer of a vast empire, and encourager of the temple rebuilders, stands in contrast with Belshazzar of ch. 5, the profligate and foolhardy desecrator of the sacred vessels. The lesson learned by one was that the God of Israel may not be spurned and sinned against with impunity; the lesson learned by the other was that this same God of destruction reaches down to rescue a man who refused to compromise the faith of his fathers. The truth of the author's theological presentation is not to be gauged by the accuracy of his historical reconstruction, for the proclamation that the God of Israel is a God of judgment and of mercy is not dependent on the historicity of 'Darius the Mede'.

1-9 Daniel's prominence in the kingdom has been integral to three earlier stories and his promotion to high office has already been referred to explicitly (2:48 and 5:29). From the gifted young man of the introductory tale in ch. 1 he has progressed to the point where he is recognised as one of a triumvirate of presidents responsible for the whole realm. Though hegemony over the region has passed from the Babylonians to the Persians, Daniel's own career has not been interrupted. Rather, because of an 'excellent spirit' (v. 3), he has been able to outstrip his colleagues and is likely to receive even further preferment. It is here, of course, that the difficulties commence, and that the plot of the story begins to take shape. This is the second time in this series of stories in which Jews have been threatened by the action of local officials. The first is recounted in ch. 3, whose points of contact with the present chapter are obvious. Not the least of these is that the earlier story, too, moves within the parameters of two royal decrees and has as its pivotal point the issue of faith and martyrdom.

The force of the verbal construction in v. 4 is such as to suggest that Daniel's two colleagues and their collaborators repeatedly monitored his behaviour in order to find some reportable offence. When all attempts in this direction proved fruitless, they were forced to resort to the setting of a deliberate trap. Ironically, what was a source of strength for Daniel, the devout observance of his faith, was now to become the means of his possible undoing. The Aramaic word translated 'law' by the RSV in v. 4 would better be rendered 'religion' in this context (see also Ezra 7:12, 14). The schemers' reference to this is not expanded, presumably so that the reader may ponder for the moment on what possible hidden cause of downfall could be found in faithfulness itself. The answer is soon forthcoming. The antagonists of the faithful Daniel display all their cunning. With one accord (cf. RSV translation and footnote) they approach Darius and put to him the proposition that he should promulgate a decree proscribing prayer to any god or man save Darius himself, for a period of thirty days. Any offender 'shall be cast into the den of lions'. As a possible means of extermination this no doubt was not an invention of the author, though it is unattested as an ancient Near Eastern practice. This well-contrived and cleverly disguised plan is presented to the king as the unanimous wish of all the prefects, satraps, and so on. Quite unaware of the real purpose of the quest, and touched by the flattery of his officials, Darius put his name to the document, and in so doing made a decision which he was later to find, to his own chagrin, was irrevocable.

It would be unwise to seek behind this depiction of an easily manipulated king any reference to actual events or real characters. Certainly to have been used in this way is out of keeping with what is known of Darius I. The accusers' plot was craftily hatched and skilfully handled, but apart from capturing the prey it could not help but bring humiliation on the king. It has an air of unreality about it, but as the plot of a story that finds its reality not in incidentals but in edifying purpose, it is not easily surpassed. With the book of Daniel Hebrew literature may be moving into the area of bizarre apocalyptic, but a place can still be found for a story whose succinct and exciting content and presentation lack nothing by comparison with the great tales of former heroes like Samson and David.

Given that the final form of the book of Daniel emerged during the fateful days of Antiochus Epiphanes, is it possible that in the figure of Darius there is some veiled reference to the Seleucid

monarch? This is most unlikely. Neither the unattractive features
of the story's king nor his undoubtedly attractive features would
permit any such identification. Had Antiochus IV, in some weak
moment, become the victim of the machinations of his officials
whereby he had issued a decree contrary to his better judgment,
he could never have been represented as regretting the harm that
had unwittingly befallen a worshipping Jew. Central to Antiochus's policy of enforced religious and cultural unification of his
kingdom was the proscription, among other things, of the very
practice which Daniel, with the tacit support of the story's king,
is determined to preserve. In its original form the story is certainly earlier than the time of Antiochus.

10-17   Daniel's response is prayer; but for him this was not the
last, desperate resource of an imperilled man. The Daniel of this
story, as of others, was not unaccustomed to praying. We are told
that it was a practice in which he engaged three times a day,
with his face towards the Holy City of Jerusalem some five
hundred miles to the west. In 9:3 he is presented in much the
same posture, though there his prayer was accompanied by 'fasting and sackcloth and ashes'.

There is little question that it is the author's intention to en-
courage faithfulness and perseverance among his own people and
that prayer is a key instrument. For him, the one effective means
of passive resistance to a political power and to a religiously
oppressive regime is prayer. There is no criterion by which to
measure the author's achievement unless it is the endurance of
the faith of Judaism whose times of testing have been as bitter
as they have been numerous. In the figure of Daniel he has most
effectively created an archetype of the praying saint. Of all the
great men and women of the Hebrew Scriptures Daniel more
than any other has kindled the imagination of traditional Jewish
and Christian art. It is rather curious, however, that the practice
developed of portraying him, not kneeling as indicated in the text
of this chapter (v. 10), but in the later traditional posture of
standing with raised hands, and again, not in the upper chamber,
but in the lions' den. For an explanation of this, one has to look
to the spate of legendary tales to which the Daniel story gave
rise.

Though in the tale itself nothing is said of the hero having prayed when in the midst of the lions, the assumption that he did so is not contrary to the spirit of the story. One midrash, that to Psalm 64, relates how Daniel failed to respond immediately to the king's anxious question (v. 20) because he was at that time reciting the Shema ('Hear, O Israel . . .'; Deut. 6:4ff.). It requires little imagination to understand how the text's silence at this point, together with the threatening martyrdom of the faithful Jew, lends itself to legendary accretion.

The custom of praying three times daily finds support in Ps. 55:16-19. One traditional Jewish source attributed it to the patriarchs (T.B. *Ber.* 26b), and another to Moses (Tanhuma *Ki.* 1). It is likely that mention of it in Daniel gave added authority to a developing practice, but praying thrice daily, despite its biblical warrant, has never been accepted as a Torah obligation. The habit of facing towards Jerusalem in prayer is attested in 1 Kgs. 8:44 and became common in the early years of postbiblical Judaism. No doubt it was this custom that was responsible for the orientation of synagogues. It is written of Daniel that he used to get 'down upon his knees', a posture that is referred to elsewhere in the Hebrew Scriptures (e.g., 1 Kgs. 8:54; Ezra 9:5; Ps. 95:6). On certain occasions the one engaged in prayer is depicted in a kneeling position and with hands spread out (Ezra 9:5). This latter practice, the spreading out of the hands without any indication of any other bodily posture, receives mention in a number of places (Ps. 28:2; Isa. 1:15; Lam. 2:19) and was emulated in both Judaism and early Christianity.

While prudence might have dictated that he remove himself a little from the public view, not least from those intent on spying on him, Daniel saw no reason to depart in any way from the practice of a lifetime. The accusers, with their task made easier by the boldness of their quarry, once more approached the king. The storyteller moves step by step through the question and answer format of the ensuing confrontation. Very deftly the king is manoeuvred into a position where he has no option but to give the command which both he and his interlocutors knew to be the sealing of his trusted servant's fate. The picture we are given of Darius is that of a man whose pride has outstripped his discernment. He has allowed a group of rather formidable yet unscrupulous and flattering retainers to force his hand and to wrest from his protection a valued official whom he was planning to

promote to the highest executive office in the land (see v. 3). He
has become the victim of his own vanity, but also of an astute
piece of political chicanery. Clearly the author wishes to invoke
some touch of sympathy for a man who is at the same time both
powerful monarch and helpless friend, caught up by the dexter-
ous manipulation of an immutable decree and desperately seek-
ing a way of escape. But there was no way out; the law must run
its course. Behind the informative note in v. 14 that the king
'laboured till the sun went down to rescue him', we are invited
to imagine the fevered activity of the court lawyers looking for
that never-to-be-found loophole. Had it been found, the story
would have lost both its point and its poignancy.

For the third time Daniel's accusers enter the presence of the
king, this time in triumph (v. 15). The hapless Daniel is arrested
and cast into the den of lions, but not before Darius offers him
one last word of hope; it may be that the God whose worship
Daniel refused to compromise will come to his rescue (v. 16). For
their part the story's villains make sure that no ordinary methods
will be used to effect Daniel's escape. The entrance to the pit was
covered with a stone, which was in turn packed around with clay
or some like substance, and sealed with the signets of the king
and his lords, so that any interference with it could be plainly
detected.

18-24 Attention is again turned to the lamenting Darius. For
him there was no alarming dream as was the case with Nebuchadnezzar, no threatening hand inscribing a message of doom
as with Belshazzar, only the painful recollection that he was responsible for the death of a good man. All kingly power had been
stripped from him; the office remained, but one unthinking action
had shorn it of all its effectiveness. He was alone in his palace,
surrounded by all the reminders of a glorious kingdom, unable
to lift a hand, unable even to sleep. It is not clear whether or not
we are to understand by the RSV use of the word 'fasting' in
v. 18 that Darius was engaged in some kind of religious activity.
It may simply mean that he had no appetite for food. 'Diversions'
could mean a number of things. It could refer to 'musicians',
'dancing girls', or some similar entertainment commonly associated with oriental courts. Or, with Rashi, the sense could be
that he spent the night without food; no table was brought to

him. Whatever the exact meaning of the Aramaic word, the gist
of the verse is clear beyond question. Darius spent a long and
lonely night, waiting anxiously for dawn to break. When at last
it did, he went with haste to the lion's den (v. 19).

The author of the book of Daniel, in his building on an earlier
story, occasionally but deliberately has a foreign monarch utter
a profoundly theological statement. Verse 20 is one such instance,
for here we find Darius, in his pained cry to Daniel, using the
telling expression, 'the living God'. That the God of Israel is such
a God, alive and not dead, enduring and not ephemeral, has to
be brought home to the author's compatriots, and how better to
proclaim that truth with unparalleled effectiveness than to have
it come from the lips of a pagan. From the midst of those whose
gods are 'gods of gold and silver, bronze . . . and stone' (5:4),
cast by a workman (Isa. 40:19), and carried on weary beasts
(Isa. 46:11), the confession arises that there is a living God, the
God of Daniel, and the God of Daniel's people. What was then
a message of hope has lost neither its cogency nor its immediacy.

Daniel's response is prefaced by the customary words of deference, 'O king, live for ever', hitherto used only by Babylonians
(2:4; 3:9; 5:10; 6:6). This, interestingly, is the first occasion in the
story when Daniel and Darius converse. So far, despite the centrality of these two, others have been able to fashion events around
them. The position each finds himself in now has been contrived
by the machinations of ambitious courtiers. But from this point
onwards the initiative lies elsewhere. Daniel informs the king of
the cause of his deliverance.

God has intervened, not immediately, but through an angel.
In preexilic texts the presence of the word here translated 'angel'
might have occasioned some hesitancy as to the most suitable
English rendering. By and large, the noncommittal 'messenger'
would be the wisest equivalent. As the postexilic period progresses, however, the hesitancy rightly disappears, and the translation 'angel' is indisputably correct in a context such as this.
The further one moves towards the end of the era, the more
developed this phenomenon of angelology becomes (see below
under ch. 8 for a fuller discussion). Daniel speaks of the cause of
his escape and also of the reason, namely, '. . . they have not hurt
me because I was found blameless. . . '. It is unlikely that Hartman is correct when he asserts that Daniel's deliverance is to be

attributed to divine justice because God 'would not permit the innocent to suffer unjustly' (*Daniel*, 200). It is true that Daniel is prepared to state his blamelessness as the reason for his own life being spared. In this immediate context Hartman's point is well taken, but in its bland generalised form, which is not restricted to this particular context, it runs counter to the tenor of the book as a whole.

Just as Mattathias's testament to his sons in 1 Maccabees praises Elijah for his great love of Torah, and Hananiah, Azariah, and Mishael for their faith, so, too, Daniel's virtue is singled out: 'Daniel because of his innocence was saved from the mouth of the lions' (1 Macc. 2:60).

A second reason for Daniel's deliverance is given in the following verse (v. 23), 'he . . . trusted in his God.' Neither innocence nor trust can be assumed to be the successful formula for rescue from persecution. The author is not fashioning a doctrine of cause and effect; his purpose is far less speculative and far more practical. The warning to his compatriots is that neither rank nor influence may be able to stem the tide of anti-Jewish fervour. Hope does not reside in any human, however powerful, but in God alone. The story of Daniel offers hope, not a remedy. The reader is asked to grasp hold of that hope not as the sure and certain means of deliverance but as an attitude to life. Any finely constructed doctrine would have foundered on the rock of present experience. Only the belief in resurrection (12:2-3) could give to the imprecision of life a more satisfying reply.

The punishment meted out to Daniel's accusers is meant to give juridical balance to the story. Of course it introduces its own difficulties, particularly when it is related in such a matter-of-fact way that not only the malefactors themselves but their wives and children were mauled to death by the lions. Whether this is to be understood as sheer vindictiveness, or the author's comment on the royal cruelty of his day, is difficult to determine. It need not be taken as the former. It may be no more than the recognition that Darius is now no longer shackled by law, but is free to act as a typical oriental potentate.

25-27 Darius's epistle has the same wide circulation as that of Nebuchadnezzar in 4:1. Indeed, the two prefacing statements, including the salutation, are identical, except for the royal name.

A further parallel is to be found in the decree issued by Nebu-chadnezzar after the miracle of the rescue from the fiery furnace (3:29). A significant difference is that, whereas Nebuchadnezzar's decree contained a threat of punishment for anyone speaking ill of the God of the three Jews, that of Darius introduces a distinc-tively positive note in requiring reverence of the God of Daniel.

It is a feature of exilic and postexilic Judaism that the appre-ciation of the universality of the God of Israel which resulted from closer and more immediate contact with the nations led to the hope, if not the expectation, that God (Yahweh) would be acknowledged by foreigners. In differing ways, and to varying degrees, this desire is expressed in a number of significant texts, among them Isa. 42:6; 49:6; 56:6-7; the book of Jonah; Zech. 14:8, 16-19; and Mal. 1:11. It should not be inferred, however, that because of the presence of this emphasis Judaism necessarily be-came a 'missionary' faith. In the generally accepted meaning of that term it is not applicable, though that is not to say that there was no room for, or acceptance of, the convert. Acknowledgement of the God of Israel does not necessarily entail conversion to that faith. The issue is much more complex than that. If it is borne in mind that the emphasis referred to above was part of the increasingly complex nature of postexilic Judaism, facile and un-warranted judgment of that faith as nationalistic and exclusivist will be avoided.

Some of the notes sounded in the Darius doxology recall sim-ilar expressions of faith in earlier chapters (2:47; 4:3, 34-35), as well as pointing to what is yet to come (7:14).

28 With this verse the first section of the book of Daniel draws to a close. Cyrus the Persian appears for the first time but not the last, for he was the monarch reigning at the time of Daniel's fourth and final vision (ch. 10). Unlike Darius the Mede, who makes no scriptural appearance beyond this present work, Cyrus is firmly embedded in biblical history. Nor is his merely an in-cidental role. He has the singular honour of being referred to as God's 'shepherd' (Isa. 44:28) and the LORD's 'anointed' (*mashiah*, Isa. 45:1), and is the subject of Isa. 41:25. When the exiles at last received permission to return to Jerusalem it was because of a decree promulgated by Cyrus (Ezra 1:1-4; 2 Chr. 36:22-23).

Those who first heard or read the words of these stories were surrounded on all sides by idolatry. In some of its guises it was most attractive. What is more, it did not make the same demands on its practitioners as did the Torah of Judaism. Many Jews of that time must have encountered the constant temptation to allow themselves to be influenced by beliefs and practices which were utterly foreign to their own tradition. There is little question that one of the main purposes of these stories was to combat idolatry in all its forms and to present the God of Israel as the sole source of power, the only deity worthy of recognition. Modern readers may not recognize in their surroundings the same enticements, yet it would be foolish in the extreme not to admit that, in some form or other, they do exist and that they are a constant challenge to faith.

THE SAINTS OF THE MOST HIGH
Daniel 7:1-28

Chapter 7 is undoubtedly important, but the attention given to it, sometimes without adequate reference to its immediate context, has often led to a one-sided emphasis on certain aspects and to the exaggeration of these out of all proportion. Central to the book of Daniel is the faith and the fate of those Jews who, under duress, placed obedience to their deity before the demands of the state. It is this that is to the fore in ch. 7, and this, too, on which interpretative effort might most rewardingly be placed, rather than on the unexpected and inexplicable emergence of an eschatological figure.

It is a matter of debate as to whether this chapter belongs with those that precede it or with those that follow. The argument in favour of the former hinges on a supposed close affinity between chs. 2 and 7 and on their sharing a common language, namely, Aramaic. The bilingual nature of the book is taken up under 2:4 and to a lesser extent under 8:1. As for the argument concerning the close affinity of the two chapters, it should be noted that, though there is some point in this, the differences between the two are much more marked than are the similarities.

Efforts to trace the various stages by which the present admixture of prose and poetic passages supposedly reached their extant form have met with little success. The material of ch. 7 is at times rather awkwardly pieced together. Furthermore, there is no clear-cut schema of vision followed almost immediately by its interpretation as is the usual pattern in, say, ch. 8. Verses 11 and 12 appear to pre-empt what is said later in vv. 23ff., and the question is rightly raised as to whether there is here some evidence of an earlier presentation. A similar difficulty is exposed when vv. 17 and 18 are compared with vv. 23-27. Some interpreters identify vv. 21-22 as a later addition. Yet, despite the awkward and halting style that the author has employed, the unity of the chapter may be confidently asserted. A close examination will show that vv. 11 and 12 form an immediate statement of judgment which might well be expected to follow closely on the substance of v. 10. Verses 17 and 18 will be seen to be an answer to Daniel's query in v. 16b and can be accounted for on stylistic grounds as a summation of the position so far reached. Verses 21 and 22 are not an addition and bear out what has been stated above regarding the breakdown of the more straightforward schema of vision and interpretation that has served the author's purpose elsewhere. It is helpful to recognize that Daniel is not awakened from his visionary dream experience until v. 28.

So far as dating is concerned, ch. 7 is a product of the period somewhere between the desecration of the temple in December 167 B.C.E. and its capture by Judas Maccabeus in December 164 B.C.E.

1 According to the author the reigning Babylonian monarch at the time of Daniel's first vision was Belshazzar, the king who appeared in ch. 5 as the profligate nocturnal reveler whose celebrations were brought to an end by the mysterious appearance of the writing on the wall. Whatever the historical difficulties that attend the name of Belshazzar, it will at least be remembered by its attachment to this, the most widely discussed chapter in the book of Daniel. The visions of Daniel span the momentous events of the collapse of the great neo-Babylonian empire and the rise of the Medo-Persian. Only twice in the second section of the book (chs. 7 – 12) is the hero referred to in the third person: here in v. 1 and again in 10:1. With these two exceptions Daniel appears in the first person. Moreover, he is no longer the interpreter of dreams and visions experienced by others, but himself the one who receives divine revelation by these means. And, as will be seen in each of the visions, an angelic interpreter is required to come to his aid.

So far as our understanding of chs. 1-6 was concerned, it was important to recognize the story genre as the chosen vehicle of communication. What the author set out to do was to provide his audience, so to speak, with material that was both instructional and hortatory. But the choice of that particular type of presentation imposed certain restrictions and led to the presence of certain difficulties. There are elements within these stories whose presence is determined less by the theological and religious outlook of the author than by the genre itself. That is part of the nature of storytelling. The modern reader should be careful not to read too little or too much into the text. Similarly, in ch. 7, as well as in some of the chapters that follow, the chosen genre, in this case that of vision-interpretation, imposes its own limitations and raises its own difficulties.

Visions may not be an everyday occurrence, but dreams are of such common experience as to remind the reader that an essential feature of the dream is its frustratingly unsystematic structure. The material in this chapter, and in those that follow, possesses a further difficulty. We are here dealing not simply with the recalling of an experienced dream, but with the author's literary production of this. The author had to move between the limits imposed by the unsystematic nature of his material on the one hand, and the required orderliness of his purpose on the other. The dream-interpretation or vision-interpretation schema is a literary device and must be understood and treated as such. The tidiness and regularity so often imposed on it is harmful to proper interpretation. An author who produced, in these circumstances, a systematic and totally coherent account would have been less than skilful. If this is borne in mind, neither too little nor too much will be expected of such material.

2-8 Daniel's night vision begins with the stirring up of 'the great sea' and the emergence therefrom of 'four great beasts' (v. 2). It is not necessary to invoke Babylonian mythology in any search for the origin of such imagery. Sufficient material is much closer to hand, for the Hebrew Scriptures themselves make frequent mention of the watery chaos, as well as the various creatures that were believed to have inhabited it. The dark waters of the deep were for the ancient Hebrew the abode of the mysterious and the threatening. This attitude he shared with his contemporaries of all cultures and perhaps with many in more recent times; for, if the early nineteenth-century paintings of Turner are any indication, it was as persistent as it was universal. To the Hebrew, the watery depths, whether in their pristine (Gen. 1:2; 7:11) or in their later historicized form (Isa. 51:10), were the allies of chaos

and the enemies of order and, consequently, of God. In the treatment of this verse, it is better to resist the temptation to identify
'the great sea' as, say, the Mediterranean, and to leave it as
evocative not only of the unknown, but of the unknowable, as
something beyond the edge of man's cognition. To identify it is
to tame it.

The agents of this stirring up of 'the great sea' were 'the four
winds of heaven', an expression which also occurs in 8:8. Whatever the earlier mythological connotation, the use of this expression here is probably meant to suggest no more than the notion
of completeness or totality. As the four corners of the earth denote
universality, so 'the four winds of heaven', in this context, be-
token the summation of power (1 Enoch 18:2-5). The beasts
themselves are of the author's own devising, but they may well
have been suggested by the monsters that appear from time to
time in the scriptural material at his disposal, e.g., Rahab
(Ps. 89:10; Job 9:13; 26:12; Isa. 51:9), Leviathan (Ps. 74:14;
Isa. 27:1), and 'the dragon' (Job 7:12; Isa. 27:1; 51:9). The use
of animal imagery was continued in later Jewish writings though
in a less spectacular form (1 Enoch 85:90; 2[4] Esdr. 11:1, 36).
Evidence of this is also found in the NT, e.g., in Rev. 13:1 where
a beast is depicted as 'rising out of the sea'.

Each of the first three beasts was said to resemble a known
animal. The first was not a lion but 'like a lion' (v. 4), the second,
not a bear but 'like a bear' (v. 5), and the third, not a leopard
but 'like a leopard' (v. 6). The use of 'like a . . .' is not inconsequential in this chapter. Each of the monsters that emerges from
the sea is roughly identifiable but each contains ancillary features
which serve to mark it off from the known. The fourth monster,
however, defies any initial classification. It is a fitting product of
the terrifyingly chaotic waste from which it emerges. Its fright-
eningly grotesque appearance and its angry, uncontrolled behaviour set it apart from all else. For the author it represents those
forces that are in defiance of order and decency. The other beasts
move in and out of the scene quite rapidly; not so the fourth. It
is this one with which he concerns himself.

The idea of four successive empires, one replacing the other,
and the fourth necessitating divine intervention, was the subject
of ch. 2 (see especially 2:31-45). In the treatment of that chapter
the four kingdoms were identified in chronological order as Bab-

ylonia, Media, Persia, and Greece (Macedonia). The same schema may be applied to ch. 7. In adopting this device the author of Daniel is following an established practice (Pss. 68:30; 80:13; Jer. 5:6).

The first beast was 'like a lion' but had 'eagles' wings'. These two features help to identify it as representing the Babylonian empire. Jeremiah uses the figure of the lion specifically of Nebuchadnezzar (Jer. 50:17), but in a general sense also of the Babylonian power (Jer. 4:7; 49:19; 50:44-46).

Once in his work he uses the symbol of the eagle for the same purpose (Jer. 49:22), and this is also found in Ezekiel (Ezek. 17:3). The text of Daniel says of this composite beast that 'it was lifted up from the ground and made to stand upon two feet like a man'. These words and those that immediately follow, 'and the mind of a man was given to it', have suggested to some commentators a link with the figure of Nebuchadnezzar as he is portrayed in 4:13-16, 28-32. This identification, which is as early as R. Saadiah Gaon according to Ibn Ezra, is by no means certain. The plucking out of the wings and the substitution of a human mind appear to denote a loss of ferocity and power, which was most certainly the case in the last decades of the once all-conquering Babylonian regime.

The second beast, which resembled a bear, is said to have stood upright ('raised up on one side'), and to have had 'three ribs in its mouth between its teeth' (v. 5). These latter may be either the remains of one of its victims, or the word 'ribs' may more suitably be translated 'tusks' or 'fangs'. Whatever the explanation, the voracity of the beast is clearly attested in the command, 'Arise, devour much flesh.' As such it was a fitting symbol for the Median empire, which is described in just such a manner in Isa. 13:17-18 (especially v. 18) and in Isa. 51:11-33. Efforts to rearrange the text of vv. 4 and 5 to make the descriptions fit more closely the characteristics of the known lion and bear not only have no textual warrant, but miss the point; they are as unhelpful as they are ingenious.

The swift-moving, hydra-headed third beast was 'like a leopard' or 'panther'. The 'four wings of a bird' may suggest the celerity with which Cyrus extended his domain, reference to which is to be found in Isa. 41:3, while the 'four heads' may suggest his claim to universal dominion (see 8:4). Here, as elsewhere in the book, the figure 'four' denotes the idea of totality. The singling out of four Persian kings in 11:2 has led some to see a similar reference here. There would appear to be a strong case for identifying the third beast not as Persia but as Greece (Macedonia). In support of this, attention is drawn to Alexander the Great's speedy worldwide conquests (the 'four wings of a bird'), and the fourfold division of the empire after his death (the 'four heads'). But two arguments may be brought against this. First, the four wings are those of a bird and would suggest a rather poor comparison with the eagles' wings of the Babylonian beast. As the greatest conqueror of the ancient world Alexander is scarcely done justice if presented in that fashion. The second point is that the schema of the nations in ch. 7 must not be interpreted independently of chs. 8 and 11. The third kingdom as Greece, and the fourth as Rome, may have become the popular formula in later Judaism and in early Christianity, but it fails to take into account the historical milieu from which this work emerged. For the author of the book of Daniel the third kingdom was that of Persia.

It is with the fourth beast that the author's real interest lies. The very full description given in vv. 7 and 8 is some indication of this, and it is supported strongly by Daniel's questions in vv. 11 and 19f. The description of the predatory monster of v. 7 may have been suited to the exploits of Alexander the Great, but as a general characterization of the Greek empire it is most likely based on the author's intimate knowledge of the ruthless policies and activities of Antiochus IV. It is made to symbolise the Macedonian-Greek empire in both its unified and post-Alexandrian diversified forms.

Not all its features, but only a few, receive attention, and of these, the focus is on its great and extensive power, unparalleled in the history of the ancient world. The regime of Alexander stretched from Macedonia in the west to the river Indus in the east, and southwards to the land of Egypt. It brought with it complete subjugation of all the nations and city-states within that vast region. The romanticism so often attached to the figure of Alexander, and fueled by the picture of his comparative youthfulness, should not be allowed to hide his single-minded ruthlessness. It is this, particularly as it was exemplified in one of his successors, that both interests and alarms the author. The territorial ramifications of the post-Alexandrian empire were both complex and enormously widespread, but it is to only one of a number of regions that attention now turns, the one governed by the dynasty of the Seleucids and extending, at the time of the author, from Syria in the north to the Egyptian border.

The fourth beast, for which there was no known likeness — so terrible and frightening was its appearance — sprouted ten horns. It is a question whether this numeral is to be taken literally or figuratively. If the former, then a list of ten Seleucid monarchs may be adduced, beginning with Seleucus I (312-281 B.C.E.) and ending with Seleucus IV (187-175 B.C.E.), in addition to the three who were uprooted by the other horn, 'a little one' (v. 8). These latter would be Demetrius, whom Antiochus IV replaced because of his absence in Rome but who was to succeed Antiochus, another Antiochus, son of Antiochus III, and Heliodorus who, though not of the royal line, was a scheming aspirant to the throne. The 'ten', if taken figuratively, may merely indicate numerical completeness.

Any interpretation of the 'ten', or of the 'three', is fraught with difficulties, but there is little doubt that the eleventh horn, also referred to in 8:9-11, is to be taken as symbolising Antiochus IV (175-164 B.C.E.). This horn had 'eyes like the eyes of a man, and a mouth speaking great things' or 'speaking arrogantly' (L. F. Hartman, *Daniel*, 203). The purpose of this description is first of all to underline the individuality of the figure referred to. No longer is the subject an amorphous empire; it is a man. For the author and his compatriots he is the persecutor of their faith and the villainous opponent of their God. The description also confirms what is said of the 'little horn' in 8:23, that he is 'brazen-faced' and 'cunningly adroit' (cf. the RSV translation). The blasphemous behaviour of Antiochus receives interpretative treatment in v. 25.

9-14 Verses 9 and 10, as well as 13 and 14, are poetry. This does not mean that there is any necessary hiatus between vv. 8 and 9, nor may one be postulated on any other grounds. There is movement from the first act of the vision in vv. 2-8 to its sequel in vv. 9-14. The beasts, all of which represent wilfully destructive forces bent on self-aggrandisement, have emerged one by one from the watery chaos. They have no further function to perform.

81

What awaits them is judgment and sentence. The scene for this is set by vv. 9 and 10. It is generally agreed that the 'one that was ancient of days' is meant to portray the deity. A similar representation of God is to be found in 1 Enoch 71:10, where he is accompanied not only by a host of angelic beings as in v. 10, but by several archangels including two who feature in the book of Daniel, Michael and Gabriel (8:16; 10:13, 21; 12:1). However much it may offend modern theological sensibilities, it was a natural projection of the biblical image of God to portray him with 'raiment . . . white as wool' and with 'hair . . . like pure wool', the epitome of purity and wisdom. The Similitudes of Enoch provide us with a close parallel (1 Enoch 46:1), while an interesting transference occurs in Rev. 1:14. There it is 'one like a son of man' whose head and hair are 'white as white wool, white as snow'. For the author of the NT Apocalypse the imagery, drawn frequently from the book of Daniel, is of greater significance than any possible identification of like figures.

Attention is now drawn to three features which have distinct links with OT thought and imagery, i.e., the 'throne', the 'judgment', and the 'books'.

The vivid description of the throne (v. 9b) owes not a little to the Merkaba vision of Ezekiel 1 and 10, with its whirling, gleaming, four-wheeled chariot which became associated with the Divine Throne in later Jewish mystical traditions of the 11th cent. and beyond. This seat of judgment with its 'fiery flames', wheels of 'burning fire', and exuding 'stream of fire' has a parallel in 1 Enoch 14:15-23, which is roughly contemporary with the extant text of Daniel. The point should be made that, although the plural 'thrones' is used in v. 9a, only one is described in vv. 9b and 10a. There was one throne of judgment and only one, as there was one Judge and only one. Nothing in the text suggests that the figure who appears in v. 13, the 'one like a son of man', has any judicial function. Care has to be taken not to read into the text elements borrowed from NT depictions of similar scenes, e.g., Matt. 19:28 and 1 Cor. 6:2. The myriads of angels who stand before the throne point back to a similar scene in 1 Kgs. 22:19 and have their counterpart in 1 Enoch 1:9; 14:22; 71:8, 13; and 91:15. They become an integral part of the divine entourage.

The notion of a judging God is commonplace in the Hebrew Scriptures. Divine judgment is prepared for Israel (Amos 2:6ff.;

7:7ff.; Mic. 6:1-8) as it is for the nations of the world (Pss. 9:7-8; 82; 98:9). Mankind, both individually and corporately, will stand before the throne. Again this becomes an essential feature of biblical eschatology. Though the Daniel text makes no explicit mention of the place of judgment, the idea that it is to be carried out on earth may not readily be ruled out. Moreover, this is not contrary to the OT record and may find firm corroboration elsewhere. God's coming to earth in judgment is mentioned in Zech. 14:5 and Joel 3:12 (RSV), and strongly suggested in Ps. 96:13. In 1 Enoch 90:20 the throne of judgment was said to have been erected 'in the pleasant land', an expression which has distinct parallels in Dan. 8:9 and 11:41, and by which is meant the area around Judea.

Integral to judgment was the opening of 'the books' (v. 10b). The OT occasionally mentions two books which appear to have had two quite different functions. One was in the form of a general record, either of what has happened, or what will happen. In Ps. 56:8-9, and again in Ps. 139:16, this is stated in personal and individualistic terms, whereas in Dan. 10:1 the 'book of truth', as it is called, contained God's plan for the nations. The other, often referred to as the 'book of life', or by some similar expression, has within its pages the names of those who have a particular relationship to God. It makes its first appearance in Exod. 32:32 and is also mentioned in Ps. 69:28 and Mal. 3:16. References to it in apocalyptic literature include Dan. 12:1; 1 Enoch 90:20; 103:2; and 108:3. Revelation 20:11-15 knows of the existence of two books, but the purpose of each is by no means clear. The presence of this notion of books containing the fate of both individuals and nations is attested in the literature of ancient Babylonia and ancient Greece, but it was sufficiently native to the Hebrew tradition to suggest that the author of Daniel had no cause to move beyond that to find his exemplars.

The judgment itself is meted out with great swiftness, but only one beast, the fourth, is said to have been destroyed. The fire which was so much a part of the imagery of the judgment throne now becomes also the agent of destruction. It would be to go beyond the plain meaning of the text (v. 11) to see here any reference to the fires of hell. This feature is singularly lacking in the book of Daniel (see 12:2) but does emerge shortly afterwards in 1 Enoch 10:6; 18:9-12; and 21:7-10. It is salutary to be reminded that not all apocalyptists thought alike. In v. 12 the fate of the other beasts receives attention. They were stripped of power but their lives were spared, at least for a while. What is meant by this is not at all clear. Perhaps there is here an oblique reference to the process by which each in turn was succeeded by another. Only the most bestial of all kingdoms, the last, is utterly destroyed, for its power is to be replaced, not by one of similar origin, i.e., the watery chaos, but by one that is the representative of God on earth. In this indistinct picture of what will occur, the three kingdoms that are spared total obliteration are the representatives of the nations that will do homage to God through his people (v. 27).

After judgment, and after the carrying out of the sentence, the 'one like a son of man' appears. Over the years, intense discussion has centred on the question of the identification of this figure. It is important to note the exact wording of v. 13. The text does not say the 'son of man' but 'one like a son of man'. In the Aramaic of Dan. 7:13 the term is *bar enash*, and in Hebrew its equivalent is *ben adam*. The latter appears frequently in the OT, especially in the book of Ezekiel (e.g., Ezek. 2:1, 3, 8; 3:1, 2, 4, 10, 17; 4:1, 16). There is little question that here it is no more than a circumlocution for the briefer 'man'. It serves to stress the humanity of the prophet as mortal man addressed by God. The *ben* indicates the classification to which Ezekiel belongs, i.e., mankind in contradistinction to any other possibility. The expression also occurs in several psalms, but its most noteworthy locale is Ps. 8:4 (RSV). Here it is clearly a parallel to 'man' in the earlier part of the verse and might best be rendered 'mortal man'. The Hebrew term is to be found twice in the book of Daniel. In 8:17 the reference is to Daniel himself. In 10:16 the plural form of *ben* is used, giving the translation, 'one in the likeness of the sons of men'. The individual spoken of is one of the angelic beings, most likely Gabriel, who comes to the aid of the distressed Daniel. Recent studies, particularly that undertaken by Geza Vermes (Appendix E in M. Black, *An Aramaic Approach to the Gospels and Acts*, 312-28), have put beyond doubt that, in its OT context at least, 'son of man', whether in Aramaic or Hebrew, refers simply to a man, and as such was not an unusual usage. The connotation of the term, of course, is extended by the prefixing of the word 'like'.

Daniel 7:13-14 says a number of things of this 'one like a son of man'. He came 'with the clouds of heaven'; he was presented to 'the Ancient of Days'; and he was the recipient of everlasting 'dominion and glory and kingdom' as well as the obeisance of the nations.

At the outset it has to be stated that these verses are part of Daniel's vision, and therefore it might be expected that they would receive attention in the interpretative section of the chapter. When this is examined it will be found that such is not the case. There is no explicit mention of 'one like the son of man' in the interpretation. Consequently, the exegete is required to find the interpretative parallel elsewhere than in this specific location. The sole possibility is in v. 27 where what is given to 'one like a son of man', i.e., 'dominion and glory . . .', is also given to 'the people of the saints of the Most High'. To neglect this specific correlation is to fail to do justice to the format and intent of the chapter. The process of identification should rightly have been concluded at this point. Some of the statements concerning the figure of v. 13, however, have not been accounted for in v. 27 and, for that matter, nowhere else in the interpretation proper. Consequently they must be examined in their own right, for presumably, if there is an alternative identification to that already stated, it must be in these statements that the clues are to be found. First of all: what is signified by the statement that he came 'with clouds of heaven'? Does this necessarily imply divinity or some like attribute? The import of the expression must be seen in its relationship or, rather, its contradistinction to what is said of the origin of the four beasts of vv. 3-8. As these emerge from the chaos of waters and represent those forces opposed to and ultimately to be destroyed by God, so the 'one like a son of man', as the chosen vehicle of God's purpose and the recipient of his rewards, comes forth 'with the clouds of heaven'. The significance of the latter words lies in the contrast that they draw, and not in any suggestion of spatial heavenly origin. The text does not say 'from heaven', nor 'on the clouds of heaven', but 'with the clouds of heaven', and this use of language must be taken seriously as no more and no less than figurative.

The next part of the act, which follows immediately on the rejection of the first three beasts, and the destruction of the fourth, is the presentation of the 'one like a son of man' to 'the Ancient of Days', i.e., to God, and the receiving of the honours mentioned in v. 14. Sovereignty has passed from the beastlike forces arrayed against God to the manlike champion of God's cause. Moreover, the transient order of past regimes will give way to the eternal order of the future. This rule of God through his people will be established when the nations do obeisance to the people who stand not in their own right but in his. The language of v. 14 recalls that of 4:3, 34 and 6:26, and is substantially repeated in 7:27. That it is not incongruous to have these words of v. 14 relate to the people of God is made quite clear by their close parallel in v. 27. Lacocque is misleading when he writes that in v. 14 'we note a new feature of the promotion of the "son of man" to divine stature' (*Daniel*, 1:147). In order to maintain this thesis he has to ascribe divinity to what he calls the 'Israelite Saints' (*Daniel*, 154). The danger in this kind of assertion is that ordinary words cease to have any ordinary meaning.

The contention that the verb *pelah* ('serve') in v. 14 is so restricted in range that it may be associated only with serving God rests on slender evidence indeed, the very infrequent use of the word, and takes no account of the possible development of language. Arguments which rely on the use of single words have little or no substance. It is not unnatural to apply the language of v. 14 to the people of God (as does v. 27). Full account must be taken of the situation from which the author of Daniel writes. Over the centuries, certainly since the early days of Nebuchadnezzar, this people had been subjected to foreign rule. Changes in ancient Near Eastern hegemony meant for Israel (the Jews) the exchange of one overlord for another. Autonomy was stripped from them; so, too, the respect of the surrounding nations. But more than this; if Israel was derided by its neighbours, so, too, was the God of Israel, for the fortunes of the one stood or fell with the fortunes of the other. There was no sign of the presence and power of God other than through the demonstration of these in his people. Verse 14 states that the situation that has befallen Israel will be removed; the roles will be reversed. Once ruled by others and spurned by their enemies, they themselves will succeed to the overlordship, and the respect hitherto denied them will be theirs. The book of Daniel is not alone in heralding this dramatic turn in the nation's fortunes. It is also to be found in

Isa. 61:5-9, which contains the promise of 'everlasting joy' (v. 7) and the establishment of 'an everlasting covenant' (v. 8). The notion of 'everlasting dominion' in Dan. 7:14 is no more indicative of divinity than is the statement of Isaiah 61. There is in both passages an extension of the thought of Joel 3 (RSV). Israel exists as the people of God, not to represent its own interests, but his. Only when this is forgotten can such a claim as is made in v. 14 be misinterpreted as the expression of a questionable nationalism.

The key to the interpretation of vv. 13 and 14 is to be found in v. 27. There is no quasi-divine figure, the 'son of man', in the Hebrew Scriptures. Recently M. Casey has argued vigorously that there is no evidence anywhere in Jewish literature of a 'son of man' concept (*Son of Man: The Interpretation and Influence of Daniel 7*, 139). No doubt the debate will continue. While the NT contains clear evidence of such a concept, it has to be categorically stated that there is no natural line of development of this from the writings of the OT.

There is no indication in Dan. 7:13-14 that the 'one like a son of man' is to be the deliverer of his people; nor is there any specifically messianic connotation. Only by the widest definition of the term 'messianic' could any other conclusion be reached. Though the archangel Michael, rather than the messiah, acts for Israel in the book of Daniel, it is also to go beyond the evidence to see any association with the former in vv. 13 and 14. The 'one like a son of man' is not the messiah, nor is he Michael, nor for that matter, Gabriel; rather, he is the personification of 'the people of the saints of the Most High'. Such interpretation does not detract from the NT's presentation of the figure of Jesus Christ. In the NT's most forceful portrayal of the redemptive aspect of Jesus' humanity and its representative nature the office of 'son of man' receives no mention (see Heb. 2:14-18 and 4:14-16). The claim of uniqueness rests not on the identification of Jesus as the fulfilment of some supposed OT concept of such a figure, nor even on messiahship, but rather on the confession that he is the Son of God. It was at that point that the cleavage between those who chose to follow Jesus and those who adhered to the traditional faith occurred. The Church could make that confession, but for the Synagogue it was, and still is, an unacceptable doctrine.

15-18 Verses 15 and 16 introduce the interpretation. The one who was himself the interpreter of dreams in chs. 2 and 4 now becomes the one who requires enlightenment, and this is forthcoming from one of the attendant angelic beings. Rather oddly, and in contrast to similar episodes elsewhere in the book, the interpretation is actually contained within the vision. The awakened Daniel does not appear until v. 28.

The explication of the vision begins with a general statement (vv. 17-18) which, though intended to serve the immediate purpose of putting Daniel at ease, succeeds only in further arousing his curiosity. The summary statement declares that the four beasts are indeed four kings (or kingdoms) and that they will be dispossessed by 'the saints of the Most High'. The words 'out of the earth' do not contradict what was said in v. 3. Rather, they indicate in a general way the origin as well as the status of the four regimes in contradistinction to the origin and status of God's people. The mention of 'the saints of the Most High' who will receive and possess the kingdom (v. 18) is the first step in the process of identification of the 'one like a son of man' (v. 13), but it itself is dependent on v. 27 for its final explanation.

The point that is made here is that the figure of v. 13 is not an individual. Though a case for the identification of the former in terms of angelic forces contending for Israel might be possible on the strength of this verse and v. 22, in the light of the conclusive evidence of v. 27 it is only tentative.

19-27 For Daniel, as for the reader of his day, the pressing issue has to do with the fourth beast, which is depicted in v. 19 as luridly as in v. 7 with the insertion of two additional features: it has 'claws of bronze' and the eleventh horn is said to have been superior to the others (v. 20).

Though vv. 21 and 22 interrupt the interpretation, they are not necessarily to be seen as a later addition. In summary form they anticipate the fuller description given in vv. 23 to 27, but in a presentation which interlaces vision and interpretation, they may be taken as an extension of the former. There is no neat vision-interpretation sequence in ch. 7.

The fourth kingdom (v. 23) is, as stated earlier under v. 8, that of Macedonia (Greece). At its height under Alexander the Great, and certainly from the point of view of a writer living in the small 2nd-cent. B.C.E. province of Judea, it did indeed 'devour the whole earth'. Interest passes quickly to the eleventh horn, which is to be identified with the arch villain of the book of Daniel, Antiochus IV (175-164 B.C.E.). The reference in v. 25a to his blasphemous words and haughty mien is confirmed in 8:10-12; 9:26-28; and 11:21-45. It was Antiochus who moved and removed high priests, who looted the temple treasury, who ordered savage reprisals against the helpless population of Jerusalem, and who erected as a sign of his authority the dreaded Akracitadel within the shadow of the temple. In addition to all this, as the opposition to his policies gained in strength, he proscribed the Torah and the sacrifices, outlawed the traditional customs, and persecuted to death those who defied these measures. By such means he sought to 'wear out [devastate] the saints of the Most High' and to 'change the times and the law'. In this programme of enforced Hellenization everything that bore the mark of traditional Judaism was uprooted, but the crowning act of blasphemy, the challenge to God himself, was the setting up of 'the abomination that makes desolate' and the offering of sacrifices to Zeus (Dan. 11:31). This occurred on 15 Kislev (6 December) 167 B.C.E., and it was not until 25 Kislev (14 December) 164 B.C.E. that the alien structure was removed, the temple cleansed, and the lights lit. The period when Antiochus's persecution was in full flight fits in tolerably well with the 'time, two times, and half a time' of v. 25b. Presumably this was three and a half years. More accurate assessments are provided at 8:14 and 12:11. There is a possibility that the expression in v. 25 is not to be taken as anything more than the indication of a lengthy period. In a number of places in the NT Apocalypse mention is made of a specific figure of forty-two months or 1260 days (Rev. 11:2, 3; 12:6, 14; 13:5). An account of the rigours of Antiochus's policy and its devastating effect on the people over the longer period from 170 B.C.E. to 164 B.C.E. is to be found in 1 Macc. 1:20-64 and another, less reliable historically, in 2 Macc. 5:1 – 6:11.

Antiochus's estimation of his own personal worth and accomplishments was such that he took to himself the epithet 'Epiphanes', 'manifestation of God'. This blatant expression of human pride, however, could not protect him from the God of the people of Israel whose purpose he had attempted to thwart. Judgment, in the end, was in the hands of a God far superior to any known to Antiochus.

In v. 27 'the people of the saints of the Most High', which extends the earlier 'saints of the Most High' and gives it a national dimension, puts the issue of the identity of the 'one like a son of man' (v. 13) beyond question. These are they who, having been persecuted, will receive from the Divine Judge honour and preferment. Not by force of arms, but by the intervention of their God, they have become the inheritors of their erstwhile persecutors.

The task the author has set himself is to instil in a denigrated and seemingly abandoned people the belief that their suffering will not go unnoticed. The reward they are to receive, cast in exaggerated terms, is a counterbalance to what they have had to endure. There is no suggestion in the text that they should be the recipients of 'cultic reverence and obedience of a religious order' (Lacocque, *Daniel*, 154). It is reasonable to assume that such an eventuality was as far from the mind of the author of Daniel as it was from the minds of his predecessors. The reference to Israel is political, but the inference to be drawn from this is that the outward recognition of the people carries with it the concomitant recognition of their God.

28 Daniel's reaction is to be seen as the natural response of a man who has been made privy to the secret counsel of God. The author's purpose is advanced and the authoritative nature of his writing enhanced by Daniel's secret storage of the divine truth in readiness for the day of its revealing. With 7:28 the Aramaic section of the book comes to a close.

THE ARCH VILLAIN
Daniel 8:1-27

To a degree ch. 8 suffers by comparison with what has preceded it. It lacks the narrative quality of chs. 2 – 6 and its pedestrian prose stands in marked contrast to the impressionistic poetry of much of ch. 7. Though it continues the use of animal imagery, it lacks the crisp, cryptic style of ch. 7. It replaces it, however, with something of equal importance. It is in ch. 8 that the first firm clues to the identity of the various kingdoms emerge. In this respect, at least, it takes pride of place within the book. Both ch. 2 and ch. 7 are dependent on it for their proper interpretation.

Chapter 8 shares its markedly inferior literary quality with chs. 10 – 12 and, to some extent, with ch. 9. There are perhaps two reasons for this. The first is that in all probability these chapters are a translation from an original Aramaic text and, as such, betray a certain clumsiness of movement from one language to the other. It is to be noted that at 8:1 Hebrew is again in use, and it continues to be used throughout the remainder of the book. The second reason is that the content of these chapters is such that it is difficult to avoid an awkward style. Most of it consists of a not heavily disguised presentation of historical details gaining in complexity the nearer it moves towards the time of the author and his first readers.

The chapter comprises a superscription and introduction (vv. 1-2), a visionary experience (vv. 3-14), an interpretation of the vision (vv. 15-26), and a conclusion (v. 27). As it stands, it shows no clear signs of disunity, but a closer examination has suggested to some scholars that there are secondary insertions, notably vv. 13-14 and 23-25. This claim is far less convincing if the single authorship of chs. 8 – 12 is accepted. For the minor exception to this see under ch. 12.

1-2 According to the superscription, the events of this chapter are to be dated some two years after the experience described in the previous chapter. We can only guess at the reason for this relatively accurate dating, though no doubt one purpose was to give to the whole work an aura of exactitude and of historical verisimilitude. The two chapters, 7 and 8, are closely related despite the wide divergency of format.

The locale of the vision is Susa, the winter capital of the monarchs of Media and Persia. Most likely we are to understand that Daniel was transported to that site as part of the visionary experience. Something similar is to be found in Ezek. 8:3 and 11:1. Hartman (*Daniel*, 224) revives the view, attributed to Saadiah, that Daniel stood, not by the river Ulai, but by the gate Ulai. This has support geographically and is textually possible.

3-14 The ram with the two horns is identified in v. 20 as 'the kings of Media and Persia'. It will greatly facilitate the treatment of this chapter if the interpretation (vv. 15-26) is applied immediately to the vision. The higher and later horn is a reference to Persia and the smaller, of course, a reference to Media. It was in the person of Cyrus II the Great that these two kingdoms were united in 550 B.C.E. At its peak this great empire stretched eastward as far as the Indian border, southward to Egypt, northward to the area of the Caspian Sea, and westward to the eastern edge of the continent of Europe. In 480 B.C.E. Xerxes I sacked Athens, though his victory was short-lived. During the reign of his successor, Artaxerxes I (465-424 B.C.E.), the power of the Persian empire began to diminish, but the general comment in v. 4 is an accurate one. A central theme of the book of Daniel is that sooner or later each earthly kingdom will meet its match and give way to another. In this the Persian empire was no exception. The Persian ram is confronted by the Macedonian he-goat (vv. 5-7). The troubles that beset Persia during the time of Artaxerxes I were greatly exacerbated by the rise of the ambitious Philip of Macedon (359-336 B.C.E.), but more particularly by the latter's son and successor, Alexander III the Great (336-323 B.C.E.). He is the 'conspicuous horn' of v. 5, though the reference to the he-goat's dramatic advance 'from the west across the face of the whole earth' is most likely a reference to the Macedonian (Greek) empire as a whole and not just to the successes of Alexander.

In 334 B.C.E. Alexander crossed the Hellespont and defeated the Persian army at the river Granicus, and in the following year Darius III was routed at Issus. By 331 B.C.E. Alexander controlled Asia Minor, Syria, Palestine, and Egypt. The decisive battle which put the heart of the Persian empire at his disposal was fought and won on 1 October, 331 B.C.E. at Guagamela, just east of the Tigris River (vv. 6-7). Although Alexander did not interfere with the Jewish faith or seek to depose the high priest, the assessment of him in 1 Macc. 1:1-4 is decidedly adverse. No doubt this judgment, written as it was about 140 B.C.E., was greatly influenced by events of the 2nd cent. rather than those of the 4th. The statement in v. 8 that he 'magnified himself exceedingly' possibly reflects a claim to divinity, and this, too, would strongly colour any Jewish evaluation of his reign. The extent of his conquests receives further brief mention in Dan. 11:3. Success attended Alexander as far east as the banks of the river Indus, but it was there that he received his first serious setback. This occurred not at the hands of an opposing force but from within the ranks of his own army. His troops refused to continue their eastward march, and so, in the year 326 B.C.E., Alexander was forced to return to Babylon. The concluding period of his reign was spent in organising and administering a vast empire. But, as v. 8 indicates, 'when he was strong, the great horn was broken'. In 323, at the age of 33, Alexander died.

It should be pointed out that this was not the first meeting of the Greek and Jewish worlds. Syria and Palestine had come under Greek economic and cultural influence long before the conquests of Alexander. Moreover, the wars between Egypt and Persia, so often fought on Palestinian soil, involved the use of Greek mercenaries in both armies. The new situation that emerged with Alexander was that Judea and its neighbours were now part of a massive empire ruled over by Macedonians.

With Alexander's death the 'great horn' was replaced by 'four conspicuous horns toward the four winds of heaven' (v. 8). The great conqueror left no eligible heir. He had two infant sons, one of whom was born to him posthumously, and a feeble-minded brother, Philip of Arrhidaeus. Though the latter lent some nominal semblance of unity to the empire it became inevitable that a division of authority should take place. The figure 'four' of v. 8 is probably meant to be no more than a round number in keeping with the 'four winds of heaven', but it is roughly correct. The wars among the successors (the Diadochi) lasted for some four decades. What is significant so far as the book of Daniel and the region of Syria-Palestine are concerned is that two formidable powers emerged, one centred in Antioch (the Seleucids of Syria) and the other in Alexandria (the Ptolemies of Egypt). During the last two decades of the 4th cent. wars between the successors to Alexander caused southern Syria and Palestine to change hands seven times. In 301 B.C.E., following the Battle of Ipsus, the national boundaries were etched in, at least temporarily, but Palestine continued to provide ample room for marching armies.

In the vision (vv. 3-14), and in the interpretation (vv. 15-26), the ram and he-goat receive minimal attention. Instead, the author's attention is focussed on the 'little horn' of v. 9. He asserts that it 'grew exceedingly great toward the south, toward the east, and toward the glorious land', i.e., Palestine. The identification of the 'little horn' with Antiochus IV, the Seleucid monarch who reigned from 175 to 164 B.C.E., is obvious, though Rashi, among others, was convinced that it was a reference to the Roman empire. A number of indications from the text suggest that the identification with Antiochus IV is exegetically sound.

What is to be made of the statement in v. 9 that it 'grew exceedingly great toward the south. . .'? It is known that in 169 B.C.E. Antiochus invaded Egypt and at first was highly successful. An expanded account of this is to be found in Dan. 11:25-30, in 1 Macc. 1:16-20, and in 2 Macc. 5:1-14. His absence in Egypt provided an opportunity for action by groups within Jerusalem who resented his interference with the high-priestly office and who wished to divest themselves of his appointee, Menelaus. The unexpected return of Antiochus from the south, however, caught the Jewish insurgents by surprise and led to severe reprisals against the populace of Jerusalem. Not for the first time, and certainly not for the last, the temple was plundered. By such means the Seleucid monarch enforced his hegemony over what the author calls 'the glorious land', an expression which has parallels in both the psalms and prophets (e.g., Ps. 106:24; Isa. 13:19; Jer. 3:19; Ezek. 20:6; Zech. 7:14). The words 'toward the east' are doubtless a reference to a later compaign (166 B.C.E.) against the Persians and the Parthians (1 Macc. 3:27-37; 6:1-7).

Verse 10 notes that 'it [the little horn] grew great, even to the host of heaven. . .'. This could be a reference to the events of 169 B.C.E. mentioned above, but in light of what follows in vv. 10 and 11 it is more likely that the author had in mind the even more catastrophic happenings of 167 B.C.E., a date of central significance in any attempt to understand the message of the book of Daniel. Again, civil unrest was the occasion for drastic Seleucid reprisals. These came at the hands of Antiochus's general, Apollonius, who approached the city as though on a peaceful mission but, taking advantage of the Sabbath, proceeded to inflict heavy loses on its inhabitants. Jerusalem itself was partly destroyed and a fortification known as the Akra, a citadel for foreign troops, a refuge for apostates, and a conspicuous symbol of Seleucid oppression (1 Macc. 1:29-40), was erected in the vicinity of the temple. There is an obvious reference in v. 10, 'and some of the host of the stars it cast down to the ground', to the 'Lucifer myth' of Isa. 14:12-20a, a description of royal pretensions that readily lent itself to the figure of the haughty Antiochus. This theme is popular among the apocalyptists and is also taken up in 1 Enoch 46:7 and in Rev. 12:7-12 where the enemy is identified with Satan. Such interpretation is not possible in the Daniel text, however. Indeed, it would be unwise to take these words as merely descriptive of some heavenly battle which rages between the forces of God and anti-God to the exclusion of the earthly representatives, on the one hand the faithful adherents to the Torah and on the other their arch-persecutor. Here, as elsewhere in Daniel, the engagement between the opposing forces is seen to take place on two levels, the heavenly and the earthly. There is a contrapuntal connection between the two, for the fortunes of the one are determined by the fortunes of the other. This is also to be found in 11:45 – 12:1.

Verse 11 commences: 'It [the little horn] magnified itself, even up to the Prince of the host'. Antiochus's ferocious policy of containment, directed physically against the Jerusalemites, was tantamount to an attack on God himself. Lacocque offers another interpretation and revives the view of the Targum to Ps. 137:7, however, and Ibn Ezra claims that the 'Prince of the host' is not God but the angel Michael, the protector of the Jewish people.

Some support can be found for this in 10:13 and 12:1, but in this context such an interpretation necessitates a strained exegesis of the remainder of v. 11. The closing section of the verse indicates that the most blatant form of attack on the deity was the despoiling of the sanctuary and the proscription of sacrifice.

The text of vv. 11 and 12 is far from certain, and consequently an accurate translation is not possible. The general sense is sufficiently clear to allow comment, however. The measures taken by Antiochus against the Jewish faith receive mention elsewhere in the book, notably 9:27, 11:31, and 12:11, and are referred to in 1 Macc. 1:54ff. and 4:38-39. A fuller account of the state's interference in matters of religious practice, and the resulting persecution, is to be found in 1 Macc. 1:56-61 and, with possible embellishment, in 2 Macc. 6:1-11. Israel had often suffered at the hands of powerful overlords, Assyrian and Babylonian, but this was the first time it had experienced religious persecution as such. 'Truth was cast down to the ground', is the verdict of the author. And those responsible were not only Antiochus and his cohorts, but some within the ranks of the Jewish people themselves. 'Many even from Israel gladly adopted his [the king's] religion; they sacrificed to idols and profaned the sabbath' (1 Macc. 1:43). What had stood the test of time, the religion of the fathers, the Yahwism of Moses and the prophets, was now itself a sacrifice, all in the name of reform. It would be inaccurate to claim that Hellenization was unattended by certain real advantages or that it was to have a totally deleterious effect on Judaism. The latter's contact with the thought and culture of the Hellenes had some decidedly beneficial effects, ironically not least in the area of apocalyptic expression. Hebrew faith, over the centuries, had displayed an ability to withstand the inroads of alien philosophies and was sufficiently robust to absorb and gain from these, refining where necessary. Contact with Canaanite culture in its formative stages, and later immersion in an Iranian environment, had not stifled the traditional faith but had in fact enhanced it. But what the faith would be hard pressed to withstand was a general proscription of its essential practices and widespread defection among the people.

Antiochus's policy of enforced uniformity throughout his scattered domains met with considerable success. As the author notes, 'the horn acted and prospered'. But what remained to be seen was whether his victory was lasting or ephemeral, whether the spirit of Judaism could be broken and remoulded to an alien cast, or whether a tenacious tradition would eventually reassert its powerful grip. For the historian of religion it might well be an example of tradition versus innovation, conservatism versus reform, but for the pious combatant of those times it was a matter of truth versus error.

Chapter 8 mentions for the first time the attending angels. Their primary role is that of elucidation (v. 13; see also 7:16). In the first part of the book Daniel himself performs this service. In this section he is the visionary, and angels interpret for him. The substance of Daniel's vision is furthered by what appears to be a conversation between two of these heavenly messengers, though the translation of the beginning of v. 13 is not without difficulties. This can also be said of the latter part of the verse, but it would be difficult to miss the essential thrust of the question, 'How long?' How long will the sanctuary be despoiled? How long will the continual burnt offering be proscribed and the forces of righteousness trampled on? These two words echo the often heard plaintive cry of prophet and psalmist. Here the question has particularly to do with the time of cessation of a specific evil, but on the lips of the apocalyptist generally it has a much wider connotation. It points towards 'the end', to that time when God will intervene, when the old world order will give way to the new (cf. Isa. 65:17). For the Jewish apocalyptist, convinced of the lordship of God over the world of his own creation and over the history of mankind, there must be an end to all those actions that thwart the divine rule; there must be an end and a new beginning. This seeming flight from reality is the only possible expression of biblical faith. This of course may not be the immediate purport of the question in v. 13, but the larger issue is never very far away and emerges clearly in v. 17b.

Verse 13 introduces the 'transgression that makes desolate' ('the abomination of desolation') which, in a similar form, appears again in 9:27. It is a reference to the Zeus altar erected at Antiochus's command on 15 Kislev 167 B.C.E., for the author and his fellow believers the darkest of all days.

The answer to Daniel's question is given in v. 14. The sanctuary will cease to function during a period of 'two thousand and three hundred evenings and mornings'. In other words, that is the total number of evening and morning sacrifices that fail to be offered, and this entails, therefore, a period of 1150 days, a little over three years. This interpretation of the text is by no means novel and may be found as early as Ibn Ezra. Similarly reckoned periods appear elsewhere in the book, namely, 7:25 (3 1/2 years), 9:27 (3 1/2 years), 12:7 (3 1/2 years), and 12:11 (1290 days).

In the attempted explication of these figures, there is not only room for disagreement but even more ample scope for the use of unbridled imagination. An immediate question is this: Are the figures to be taken at face value, i.e., as simply indicating 'days', or, by the application of a prescribed but unstated factor, is the reference not to 'days' but to 'years'? There could be some warrant for the latter in light of the Danielic reinterpretation of Jeremiah's seventy years of exile. (On this see under 9:2 and 9:24.) From time to time both Jewish and Christian commentators have opted for this rather attenuated explication of v. 14, and it has had particular appeal for those who have sought to relate this material to the Roman empire or some later regime. If, however, the interpretation is limited to certain events within the reign of Antiochus IV, a satisfactory and eminently sensible solution is possible. On this understanding the 1150 days is seen to be a purposefully more accurate prediction than the three and a half years of 7:25. This figure was obtained by the rather neat division of the final week of years (9:27) into two equal parts. The author has experienced the desecration of the sanctuary and the proscription of sacrifices (167 B.C.E.), and is sufficiently aware of the progress of the Maccabean revolt to be able to prognosticate the end of the period of suppression. That his suggested figure of 1150 days proved to be inaccurate is attested by the correction made to it in 12:11. This, admittedly, is a most imaginative approach to a problem replete with all kinds of fascinating possibilities, but that alone may not be sufficient grounds for rejecting it. Indeed, this interpretation, which is at least as early as Ibn Ezra (12th cent. C.E.), and which is accepted by the vast majority of commentators, accords so well with what is known of those fateful Antiochian years that its commonsense solution more than atones for its banality.

15-26 With these verses the account moves from vision to interpretation, some of the points of which have been anticipated in
what has been written above. Something of the author's intended
effect can be recognised by referring first of all to the concluding
verse of the chapter, v. 27. After the experience of the vision,
which, despite the aid of the angelic interpreter, he failed to
understand, Daniel was so dismayed and distraught that he lay
ill for several days. From the position of those who are safely
removed from the action of tyrants and protected from the threat
of martyrdom, we are not readily given to appreciate the situation
of those for whom these words were written. Apocalyptic was
born of catastrophe, and those to whom it was initially addressed
were the potential victims of that catastrophe. For them the failure to understand the purposes of God, even when these were
communicated in some way to them, must itself have been a
nearly intolerable burden. Daniel's plight in ch. 8 was no private
and isolated ordeal. It was the experience of every pious Jew
who, during the dark years of Seleucid oppression, sought response to questions that were not simply academic but real and
vital, questions of life and death. Something of the mystery as
well as the burden of the hidden, of what is revealed in part only
in apocalyptic, is transmitted through the discreet use of oblique
expression and veiled reference. This is what Daniel had become
caught up in.

The one who stood before Daniel, and who had 'the appearance of a man' (v. 15), was part of the great horde of angelic
beings of the Scriptures and later Jewish and Christian writings.
That some of them had names we learn for the first time in v. 16
where such a one, Gabriel, is pressed into service at the divine
command. This development beyond anonymity is not surprising. In the book of Zechariah the angels begin to take on individuality (Zech. 2:1; 4:1; 5:5). The one mentioned in Mal. 3:1
has the descriptive appellation, 'the angel of the covenant'. At a
later stage in the book of Daniel the angel Michael is singled out
as 'your prince' (10:21) and, more particularly, as 'the great
prince who has charge of your people' (12:1), i.e., the champion
of Israel. In like manner, both Persia and Greece are said to have
had their angelic patrons (10:13, 20). This concept of national
angels could find some support in the LXX translation of

Deut. 32:8. In postbiblical Jewish literature there is a decided development of angelology (1 Enoch 20:1-8; 2[4] Esdr. 4:1 and 4:36, where other names appear). The book of Daniel is a stage in this development, and its late date is further attested thereby.

Though sufficiently remote from the area of divinity to allow no ready lapse into a crude polytheism, the angelic beings were nevertheless far removed from the realm of man regardless of how their appearance might be described from time to time. This accounts for Daniel's reaction in v. 17a, the author's pointed reference to his mere humanity in v. 17b by use of the expression 'son of man', an indirect form of address found in the book of Ezekiel (e.g., Ezek. 2:1; 3:1; 4:1; 5:1; 6:2). (See under 7:9-14 above.)

In the same verse Daniel is assured that his vision has to do with 'the time of the end', a more vague and probably more deliberately suggestive reference than that of v. 19. Though explicit reference to what the future holds has to await the reassuring words of 12:1-4, this larger issue lies just below the surface. It was, after all, one of the essential ingredients of literature of this type.

The frailty of Daniel's humanity is again to the fore in v. 18. Similar experiences are described in Dan. 10:9; 2(4) Esdr. 5:14-15; 10:29-33; and Rev. 1:17. This is more than a mere apocalyptic convention and has little or nothing to do with the state of visionary awareness (contra Lacocque, *Daniel*, 169). It emerges from the premise that such is the weakness of man that, unaided, he may be overcome by a paroxysm of fear when face to face with the revealed word of God. Who is Daniel that he can keep his feet in such a circumstance? There is in apocalyptic literature this occasional but important reminder that man's destiny is dependent on a power outside himself. Even the battles in which he is victorious have been fought for him on a higher level.

An important expression, central to the theology of the apocalyptist, occurs in v. 19: 'at the latter end of the indignation'. A similar reading is found in 11:36: 'till the indignation is accomplished'. The RSV translation 'indignation' is less than satisfactory. More suitable to this context is 'fury' or 'anger' or, better still, 'wrath'. Who or what is the source of this wrath, and what is to be understood by it? There is little doubt that what is being spoken of is the wrath of God which, so far as its end is concerned, is predetermined. The writings of Trito-Isaiah, Haggai, and Malachi include clear indications of widespread failure on the part of certain important sections of the people. In later times, this was felt so strongly that there developed the view that the whole period of the Second Temple was one of religious declension. This was in fact a comment on the priesthood rather than on the population at large. It comes through most clearly in the opening section of the Damascus Rule of the Qumran community (CD), and is also present in 1 Enoch 89:72 – 90:12. Whether or not the author of Daniel agreed entirely with this judgment on the previous four centuries is impossible to determine, but he does suggest that the wrath of God is about to reach its climax. As in the past God used Assyria as the rod of his anger (Isa. 10:5), so now, in the last days, he is using Antiochus to purify and refine his people. And as Assyria overstepped the mark in the 8th cent. and paid the penalty for so doing (Isa. 10:15-19), just so will Antiochus behave, and these excesses will bring destruction on his own head. (See v. 25b and 11:25.)

Gabriel's interpretation makes only brief mention of the kingdoms of Media and Persia (v. 20). Even Alexander the Great serves as no more than an introduction, first to the events that followed immediately upon his death, and then to the emergence of 'a king of bold countenance, one who understands riddles . . .' (v. 23). It is the latter who is represented as the acme of imperial pretension and the personal embodiment of all iniquity. The RSV translation of v. 23 can be improved on. The two expressions used to describe Antiochus Epiphanes might better be rendered 'brazen-faced' and 'cunningly adroit'. The Seleucid monarch's propensity for double-dealing is attested in his manipulation of those who coveted the office of high priest, Jason and Menelaus (2 Macc. 4:7-26). Verses 23-25 of ch. 8 are in some measure an interpretative elaboration of vv. 9-12, but they go beyond the content of the vision. This is just one point where the strict vision-interpretation format breaks down, and where it is seen to be nothing more than a literary device. In the hands of the apocalyptist it is a most effective means of communication, but it is not subject to the limitations of any particular literary form.

The text, translation, and consequently the meaning of vv. 24 and 25 are not at all clear. In v. 24 the RSV omits 'but not with his power', regarding it as a repetition of the concluding words of v. 22. If it is retained in the text it would suggest that the rise of Antiochus was not due primarily to his own efforts but in order to serve some larger purpose, namely, the will of God (so Ibn Ezra). This is in keeping with what has been said above under v. 19 (see also 1:2). The same verse makes mention of the king's great success. No doubt this is a reference to his many territorial gains, but it is also a reference to the successful winning over of some Jews to his policies. There were those among the inhabitants of Jerusalem, representatives of the more powerful stratum of society, who 'joined with the Gentiles and sold themselves to do evil' (1 Macc. 1:11-15). Furthermore, v. 24c says that Antiochus will 'destroy mighty men and the people of the saints'. Here again there is cause for disagreement with the RSV translation and ample room for varied opinion so far as interpretation is concerned. Lacocque (*Daniel*, 165) prefers to take 'the people of the saints' in apposition to 'mighty men'. Rashi understands 'mighty (men)' to be many nations. What seems to be clear is that among those who will fall victim to the power of Antiochus will be some of the faithful, 'the people of the saints'. The faith of Judaism will not be without its martyrs.

The success that attended Antiochus is again the subject of v. 25. By persuasion, by deceit, by every known ruse, as well as by force of arms, the king managed to further his own ends. With boundless conceit ('and in his own mind he shall magnify himself'), he even dares to engage in combat with God himself. It is at the point of stating this act of gross human pretension that the author begins to entertain the notion of Antiochus's fall. 'By no human hand he shall be broken': this is not so much a prognostication of what will occur as a plain statement of what is inevitable. Raised up by God, or at least allowed by God to prosper, for a purpose beyond his own knowing, Antiochus must surely be brought down by that same power. For the author, whatever the outward cause of the king's death, its accomplishment was not of any man's doing but of God's. For later accounts of what befell Antiochus see 1 Macc. 6:1-16 and 2 Macc. 9:5-29. In his understanding of God's righteous purpose, unfolded in Israel's history and in Israel's relations with the nations, the author of Daniel is a disciple of the great prophets. In his comprehension of the inevitability of the fall of the proud and haughty, he stands in the line of succession of the sages of the traditional wisdom movement. In those matters where he went beyond both, he was a child of his own times, breaking new ground, helping to foster a new method of theological expression, and writing out of the depths of a persecution not hitherto experienced by his people.

In the closing verse of the interpretation (v. 26) Gabriel assures Daniel of the veracity and truthworthiness of the revelation he has received. What has been told him will indeed happen, but he must not spread word of it abroad. It is to be hidden, to be kept under seal. By this means, a word ostensibly heard during 'the third year of the reign of King Belshazzar' (v. 1) is made to await the light of another day, a day for which it is singularly apposite and desperately necessary. Daniel thus becomes one of the guardians of the secrets of 'the end' (cf. Rev. 22:6-10 and 2[4] Esdr. 12:36ff.).

CHAPTER 9

PROPHECY REINTERPRETED
Daniel 9:1-27

Though ch. 9 contains unmistakable elements of a visionary experience (vv. 20-22), it is clearly different in type and format from what precedes it (ch. 8) and what follows it (chs. 10 – 12). There is no neatly balanced vision and interpretation sequence. Rather, what we find is Daniel pondering a prophetic text, engaging in extensive prayer, and receiving illumination on the text from the angel Gabriel.

The outline of the chapter is:
Verses 1-2 Superscription and introduction
Verses 3-4a Introduction to the prayer
Verses 4b-19 The prayer
Verses 20-23 The intervention of Gabriel
Verses 24-27 The interpretation of the Jeremianic text

1-2 Once more mention is made of the enigmatic Darius the Mede, who first appeared in 5:31 as the conqueror of Babylon, and then in 6:1 as the monarch at the time of Daniel's confrontation with the Babylonian government officials. The further detail given here is that he was 'the son of Ahasuerus' (Xerxes). The mystery of the identity of this supposed monarch is somewhat deepened by the fact that the Darius I of ancient Near Eastern historical record, who reigned from 522 to 486 B.C.E., was in fact the father of Xerxes I. This inversion of relationships further compounds a vexing problem. (For discussion of this see the introductory notes on ch. 6.)

Both vv. 1 and 2 commence with the words 'in the first year', and the omission of these in v. 2 of the Theodotion text and one LXX manuscript might suggest that it was a case of dittography. But that may not necessarily have been so. The new material introduced in ch. 9 has to do with the length of the Exile, and the setting of the chapter is sometime soon after the fall of Babylon. The author's repetition of the opening words may have been his way of indicating that it was then that hopes of return had begun to run high but, with the passing of each day, then also when disappointment would be most acutely felt. It was a time when those conversant with the words of the prophets would have been driven back to these for new light on an otherwise inexplicable situation. Indeed, this is the picture we are given of Daniel in v. 2. The conqueror of Jerusalem has been defeated, the prediction has seemingly been fulfilled, but why the delay? Daniel's eye lights on two passages in the book of Jeremiah, 25:11-14 and 29:10-14. Each of these indicates a termination of exile after seventy years, coinciding with the fall of Babylon. Some further word was due unless all hope were to be lost. Daniel might well have been inspired by his reading of the words of Jer. 29:15: 'The LORD has raised up prophets for us in Babylon'. There are two important features of v. 2 which, though incidental to the chapter's main purpose, are nevertheless of central importance for an understanding of the developments that were taking place within the Judaism of the 2nd cent. B.C.E. Both of these also have significance for later Judaism and for Christianity.

The first arises from the mention in v. 2 of 'the books', maybe more correctly, 'the Books'. This is the first and only time that this near-technical term is used in the Hebrew Scriptures. The reference in this context is most likely to the prophetic literature only, i.e., to the second part of the later Hebrew canon. By the time of composition of the extant book of Daniel it would appear that two sections of the later canonical Hebrew Scriptures had received a measure of authority and even of official acceptance. This would have been particularly so in the case of the Torah, the Pentateuch. Its new-found status owed not a little to the authoritative action of Ezra in the early 4th cent. B.C.E. But there are indications in the book of Ecclesiasticus (the Wisdom of Jesus the Son of Sirach), both in the Prologue dating from ca. 130 B.C.E. and in the book itself dating from ca. 180 B.C.E., that the prophetic collection also enjoyed at least semi-official status. To all intents and purposes the prophetic section of the later canon was closed. The development of a halakhic approach to the Torah (regulative of life and practice) helped to bring prophecy as such to a close. What the apocalyptist brought to this situation arose from his conviction that, as one living in the end times, he was not only the legitimate descendant of the prophets, but was endowed with a measure of inspiration matching that of his predecessors. His difficulty was that he could not hope to gain an audience unless he wrote pseudonymously, adopting the name of a past hero of the people.

The second of the two important features of ch. 9 is this. Out of the combination of old word and new situation arose a new literary genre, the *pesher*. Examples of this are to be found in Daniel (e.g., 9:24; 11:35; 12:3), as well as in a number of other second-century texts, among them the Testament of Moses and Jub. 23:16-32. Parts of the former are a reinterpretation of Deuteronomy 31 – 34, while the latter bears a similar relationship to the material of Genesis 25. This use of phrases from the erstwhile canonical literature, and their application to contemporary events and circumstances, is a feature of much of the apocryphal and pseudepigraphal literature and is also to be found in the NT.

3-19 Verse 3, together with v. 4a, forms an introduction to a prayer which extends to v. 19. Daniel's status as a man of prayer has already been referred to (see under 6:10-17). The required disposition for prayer is fasting and repentance, the donning of sackcloth, and the sprinkling of ashes. References to these latter practices are common in the OT (e.g., sackcloth — 2 Kgs. 6:30; Isa. 58:5; 1 Chr. 21:16; ashes — Neh. 9:1; Esth. 4:3-4). The example of fasting was set by none other than Moses himself (Exod. 34:28). For the author of Daniel, the truth of the word of God could not be arrived at without the proper frame of mind, nor could the Revealer of that word be approached without a contrite spirit.

It is likely that the prayer itself (vv. 4b-19) is not original. The arguments for this have to do with the repetitive nature of the introduction, the conclusion, the language (which is not a translation from Aramaic but the original Hebrew), and the use of the tetragrammaton (YHWH) in vv. 4, 8, 10, 13, and 14 (twice). While the tetragrammaton is also used in v. 2, i.e., outside the poem itself, this is no strong argument in favour of the poem's originality. The limitation of the use of the divine epithet to this chapter alone requires explanation, and its appearance in

v. 2 may stem from the author's recollection of prophetic texts
where the tetragrammaton is very much to the fore. Nevertheless,
whatever its source, the prayer is not at all incongruous in its
present setting. In composition it is an anthology containing a
number of quotations from Deuteronomy and Jeremiah, two books
which lend themselves admirably to such use. It is perhaps a
mosaic, but then a mosaic may also be a work of art. Within it
is a strong note of confession, less embracingly a confession of
faith than Neh. 9:6-38 (Heb. 9:6 – 10:1), but more demonstrably
a confession of sin than the latter.

The prayer in its opening verse (v. 4b) gathers up some of the
statements and nuances central to Hebraic faith. God is 'great
and terrible' (Deut. 7:21; 10:17). Expression is also given to the
covenantal bond between God and his people (Exod. 20:6; Deut.
5:10; 7:9, 21; Neh. 1:5). It is this bond, together with unswerving
acceptance of the integrity of God, that provides the author of
Daniel with his one sure ground for hope.

In v. 5 verbs descriptive of Israel's past waywardness are piled
one on top of the other. We have 'sinned', 'done wrong', 'acted
wickedly', 'rebelled', and 'turned aside'. It reads almost like a
lexicon entry, yet this effusive confession of past misdemeanours
was not without some basis. In the long history of the nation
there were times when overt wickedness and the spirit of rebellion
were so much a part of national behaviour, particularly among
the leaders, that the future looked miserably bleak. Not all was
darkness, but in a prayer of this nature these moments were
recalled. It is this transparently honest record of its relationship
with God that has given Israel's enemies a stick with which to
beat it. No other nation has provided the world with such a
devastating catalogue of its own sins. The people's failure to hear
and to heed the divine word is a constant charge throughout the
prophetic literature. In particular the allusions in v. 6 to past
recalcitrance recall the words of Jeremiah (e.g., Jer. 7:25; 25:4;
26:5; 29:19). The apostasy of Antiochian times, the period of the
book's author or redactor, had its precursors in the homage paid
to the golden calf in the wilderness (Exod. 32:1-6) and in the
recognition given the Canaanite *baalim* (Hos. 2:1-13). From the
highest in the land ('our kings') to the ordinary citizen ('the
people of the land'), Israel had turned a deaf ear to the preaching
of the prophets.

The contrasts given in v. 7 are much more succinctly expressed in Hebrew. In each case only two words are required.

Yours . . . honour

Ours . . . dishonour

This is the refrain which in one form or other is the central cry of the first part of the prayer (vv. 4b-14). The confession is personal but also national; it befits those who remain in Judea as well as those who form the diaspora (v. 7). Yet, if the *tsedaqah* of this same verse, God's righteousness, is the divine measure of Israel's 'dishonour', the 'mercy and forgiveness' of v. 9 are the measure of God's grace, and it is to this that the prayer makes its appeal.

The language of v. 10, equating 'the voice of the LORD our God' with the preaching of 'his servants the prophets', and the use in v. 11 of the technical expression 'the law [Torah] of Moses' indicates a late date of composition. This is supported by the use of the expression, 'the curse and oath which are written' (v. 11), a reference no doubt to the corpus of the Torah, most likely in its pentateuchal form.

If vv. 4b-11 are in the main a confession of sin, what follows in vv. 12-14 constitutes a confession of God's autonomy. He has every right to act as he has, especially in light of repeated warnings. Even the near-inconceivable, the destruction of the Holy City of Jerusalem, has to be accepted as a just act. In this, the words of the book of Lamentations are recalled:

'The LORD is in the right,
     for I have rebelled against his words. . .' . (Lam. 1:18a)

The LORD has done what he purposed,
     has carried out his threat. . . . (Lam. 2:17a)

The author of Lamentations wrote, of course, of the fall of Jerusalem and the destruction of the First Temple in 587 B.C.E. The Danielic confession, in an earlier form, may well have had those same events in mind, but in its present context the reference is not to a disaster of the 6th cent. but to events of the 2nd cent. There has not been the appalling devastation of those earlier days, so graphically illustrated in Lamentations, but the city has known, since the days of Antiochus IV, plundering, pillaging, suppression, and murder. Physically the Second Temple still stands, but it has been stripped of all association with the worship of the God of Israel. The sacrificial system has been proscribed by royal fiat, and the very atmosphere polluted by the presence of the alien altar to the Olympian Zeus (Dan. 11:31; 12:11; 2 Macc. 6:1-2). In the days of Jeremiah there were those who saw the temple as a protective talisman against all possible harm. It was the prophet's task to inform them that no such prophylactic or antidote existed. Disaster must inexorably follow hard on their blatant disobedience (Jer. 7:1-7). Now a distant disciple of the prophet has to refer his people to the word of that same God whose judgment they had sought to turn aside. The prefatory 'as it is written' of v. 13 developed into a formula that was to become a central feature of later Jewish and Christian exposition. Interpreters searched for a warrant for what they had to say, and found it in that brief but commanding phrase.

The supplication (vv. 15-19) begins with a recital that recalls one of the great formative events of Israelite faith, the deliverance from Egypt. In one form or another this was uttered on numerous occasions, both to extol the God of grace and to challenge his people to a fitting response (e.g., Exod. 20:2; Deut. 6:21; 26:8; Josh. 24:6; Mic. 6:4; Neh. 9:9-11). Here it immediately precedes a profession of guilt and a petition for mercy (vv. 15b-16), in the hope that the city of Jerusalem may be spared. If God will not act on behalf of his people, so the prayer continues, then let him act for his own sake (v. 17). Let him shine with favour on the desolated sanctuary. The reference of course, here and in v. 18, is to the situation described in 8:13; 9:26; 11:31; and 12:11. The plea to God is made on the grounds that the city is his; it exists to honour his name. But more than that, there is the admission that those who call on him have no righteousness of their own whereby he might be moved to deliver them. The sole basis of their approach is the mercy of God (v. 18). The centrality of the grace of God is a marked feature of Hebraic faith, not only before the Exile but in the postexilic period as well, a point not always recognised by commentators. The portrayal of the religion of this time as one of narrow particularism and arid legalism is an unfortunate and offensive caricature.

The climax of the prayer is reached in v. 19:

'O LORD, hear;
O LORD, forgive;
O LORD, give heed and act'.

In the MT it is brevity itself, seven words only, but in these seven words is the plea of a nation burdened by past sins, and stricken by a ruthless oppressor. They are also clear reminders of great prayers of earlier and happier days, notably those in 1 Kgs. 8:30, 34-39 and Ps. 5:1-2, but there is nothing with which to compare the compelling urgency of v. 19. To call it 'the Kyrie Eleison of the O.T.', as Montgomery has (*Daniel*, 368), is to impose a criterion from an alien tradition. Daniel 9:19 must be allowed to speak in the name of the faith that gave it utterance.

The links between this prayer and earlier writings within the Hebrew Scriptures have been alluded to from time to time and have been given fuller treatment in the major commentaries. What remains to be pointed out is the ongoing tradition of such prayer. There is a particular affinity with the words of 1 Bar. 1:15 – 3:8, which is probably from a time just a little later than that of the book of Daniel, and with a liturgical fragment from Qumran, The Words of the Heavenly Lights, which may be dated mid-2nd cent. B.C.E.

20-23 The long prayer has succeeded momentarily in diverting the reader's attention from the central purpose of the chapter, the reinterpretation of a Jeremianic prediction. Nothing is said of Daniel's locale on this occasion, but we are informed that his prayer was offered 'at the time of the evening sacrifice' (v. 21), i.e., in the middle of the afternoon. Antiochus has succeeded in suspending the sacrifice but he is quite unable to stifle the prayer of the faithful. Again, as in chs. 3 and 6, we witness a limit to the power of the monarch. Daniel's concern is for what has happened to the sanctuary of his people, the place on which God put his name (Deut. 12:5), 'the holy hill of my God' of v. 20. This feeling for Mt. Zion he shares with the psalmist and with the later prophets (Pss. 2:6; 3:5; 15:1; 43:3; 99:9; Isa. 27:13; 56:7, 13; 65:11; 66:20). But his prayer is interrupted by the sudden appearance of 'the man Gabriel' (v. 21) or, better, the 'manlike' Gabriel, who is immediately identified in the text as the one 'seen in the vision at the first'. This could be a reference to ch. 7, but more likely it refers to ch. 8 where Gabriel is actually named (8:16).

Daniel's guardian angel explains that he has come forth to impart 'wisdom and understanding' or, with Hartman, 'clear understanding' (v. 22). Thus Daniel joins the ranks of those who are privy to the secrets of the divine council. Moreover, he learns that he is 'greatly beloved', the recipient of a privileged status, no doubt in recognition of the faithful obedience exemplified in the earlier stories (see also 10:11). As such his prayers are heard, for from the beginning of his supplication a word went forth to summon Gabriel to his task (v. 23). And the task, of course, is to apprise the puzzled Daniel of the real meaning of the text that had caught his attention (v. 2).

24-27 The solution to the problem, at least as supplied by Gabriel, is a relatively simple one. The seventy years predicted by Jeremiah are not to be taken at face value. The real meaning lies below the surface. This is the hallmark of apocalypticism. For the divinely enlightened, in this instance, it is not merely seventy years but seventy weeks of years. There is not a hint of this possibility in the original prophecy, nor is there any readily available coefficient that may be applied to arrive at the figure of 490. It comes only as the result of fresh inspiration, divinely ordained. This is the secret and the stance of the apocalyptist. A little simple mathematics shows that the period of seventy years' exile, as presaged by Jeremiah, was fairly close to the mark. If the official end of the Exile is taken as the year of the fall of Babylon (539 B.C.E.) or the year of Cyrus's decree (538 B.C.E., Ezra 1:1-4), the beginning, on a seventy-year reckoning, would be set somewhere around 608 B.C.E. This comes within the period between the fall of Nineveh (612 B.C.E.) and the likely date of the utterance of Jeremiah's prediction (605 B.C.E.). As a 'round figure' prognostication Jeremiah's prophecy was quite accurate. For the apocalyptist, however, the difficulty lay not in the accuracy or near inaccuracy of Jeremiah's words, but in the fact that the expected state of bliss that was to follow on the return from exile did not eventuate. The nation that lost its independence in 587 B.C.E. did not regain it in 539. It merely changed one overlord for another, then another, and so on. While the yoke of Babylon had been removed, in keeping with the prophecy, a new and often more uncomfortable one was waiting to be fixed. Moreover, the diaspora did not draw to a close with the return of Zerubbabel, nor even with that of Ezra and Nehemiah. Alexandria, Babylon, and Antioch did not give up their Jews. Yet, on the basis of Jer. 29:10-14, there had been every reason to expect that at the end of seventy years the exiles would have been gathered in and the fortunes of the nation restored. Had not the preaching of the exilic Deutero-Isaiah also given good grounds for optimism? Across the wilderness a great highway was to take the triumphant procession of returning exiles back to Jerusalem where once again the presence of God would be proclaimed in the midst of his people (Isa. 40:3-11). By this token, not only would Israel be restored but it would become a 'light to the nations', proclaiming the deliverance of God to the ends of the earth (Isa. 49:6b).

Such was the expectation, but what was the reality? Far removed from the picture of triumphal return were the bands of straggling refugees, the survivors of Israel's second 'long march'. Many of their compatriots had remained in Babylonia, preferring the discomfort of exile to the dangers of a new wilderness. Those who did return had their remaining enthusiasm sapped by what confronted them — a derelict city, an alien population, hostility and resentment on all sides. But even worse was the sight of the ruined temple, a spectacle they had to live with for a generation. The prophet Haggai (ca. 520 B.C.E.) paints a picture of abject despondency: even the harvests failed; the earth itself refused to help (Hag. 1:6). What we learn from the books of Ezra and Nehemiah is scarcely more heartening. Constant internecine strife gave way in time to the threat of armed aggression as successive Seleucid and Ptolemaic rulers throughout the 3rd cent. battled for the strip of land that separated their home territories.

It is out of a despair bred by such circumstances as these that apocalypticism was born, with its optimistic thrust towards a day when the kingdom of righteousness would be ushered in. The seventy years of Jeremiah explained nothing. It made little or no sense in such a situation. But if not the seventy years, then what? The time was ripe for speculation. The so-called 'Letter of Jeremiah', composed not long after the death of Alexander the Great, proffered the suggestion that the Exile would extend for 'seven generations' (Letter of Jeremiah v. 3). How many more revisions of the original appeared is impossible to say. Few records of the

time have survived. Of those that did survive, the most important is the book of Daniel, whose words have been accorded an
authority which, even to this day, has kept alive the question:
How long?

The remaining words of v. 24 stand as a parallel interpretation
to Isa. 40:1-2. For the anonymous exilic prophet the guilt of Israel
would be requited within the comparatively short period of the
official Exile:

> Speak tenderly to Jerusalem,
>   and cry to her
> that her warfare [or 'time of service'] is ended,
>   that her iniquity is pardoned,
> that she has received from the LORD's hand
>   double for all her sins.

According to Dan. 9:24 a far longer period is set for sin and
trangression to run its full course. The verse contains a series of
three sets of parallels:

1. to finish the transgression, to put an end to sin,

2. to atone for iniquity, to bring in everlasting righteousness,

3. to seal both vision and prophet, to anoint a most holy
   place.

The first instance of parallelism is descriptive of the years that
have passed; the second contains the promise of expiation and
well-being; the third introduces the note of apocalyptic expec-
tancy. The progress is from disobedience, to absolution, to bless-
ing and fulfilment. The language offers opportunity for all kinds
of speculative treatment and, together with the succeeding verses,
has provided ample room for those unwise enough to take up the
challenge.

Some details in v. 24 require attention. The expression 'to
bring in everlasting righteousness' might better be translated 'to
bring in everlasting justice' if the strict parallelism is to be maintained, despite the fact that this is the sole occurrence of such a
notion in the Hebrew Scriptures. 'To seal both vision and prophet',
or 'to confirm the prophetic vision', is not a reference to the
cessation of prophecy. In this context it has to do with the subject
matter of Jeremiah's words. Perhaps it is scarcely necessary to
add that, contrary to earlier Christian exegesis, the words trans-

lated 'to anoint a most holy place' in the RSV have no messianic connotation. Their reference is either to the rededication of the temple itself or the altar of burnt offerings (see 1 Macc. 4:36-59). The one text, 1 Chr. 23:13, that is cited in support of an interpretation in terms of a person (a messiah) or persons (the faithful) is very slender support.

Verses 25-27 are the key to the chapter, if not to the whole book. For those who see the book of Daniel as essentially predictive, i.e., composed during the 6th cent. B.C.E., and having to do with the presaging of future events, the foretelling of the rise and fall of empires, these verses offer a wealth of possibilities. For those who reject that approach several optional interpretations remain, but they are circumscribed by the need to relate these words to the time of the writer, i.e., the 2nd cent. B.C.E. This approach takes the stated periods seriously, but regards them as coming within an overall time span that stretched from the age of Jeremiah to that of Antiochus IV Epiphanes. They can be accounted for quite satisfactorily without recourse to highly imaginative procedures. The issue between these two modes of interpretation does not hinge on whether or not it is possible for a biblical author to be able, with divine guidance, to predict events a considerable distance ahead. That possiblity is not in dispute. Rather, the point at issue is whether the substance of material such as is found in the book of Daniel was, first and foremost, a sustaining word of God to those to whom it was first addressed. It is the same type of issue that emerges from the claim that chs. 40−55 of the book of Isaiah are from an exilic prophet who spoke them, or wrote them, for the immediate comfort and strengthening of people who shared his exile.

The 'seventy weeks of years' has a threefold dimension:

1. Seven weeks, i.e., forty-nine years, from the proclamation of the word regarding restoration to 'the coming of an anointed one, a prince . . .'.

The 'going forth of the word' (v. 25) could refer to the date of the oracle in Jer. 29:10-11, i.e., 594 B.C.E., or the date of the final collapse of Jerusalem and the destruction of the temple (587 B.C.E.). Most commentators favour the latter of these two dates. In answer to the question, who is 'the anointed one, a prince

. . .'?, there are three possible answers, namely, (a) Cyrus, who is described in Isa. 45:1 as the LORD's anointed, (b) Zerubbabel ben Shealtiel, the governor of Judah after the Return, with Jeshua responsible for rebuilding the altar and temple (Hag. 2:21-23; Zech. 4:6-14; Ezra 3:2) and one of the two anointed referred to in Zech. 4:14, and (c) Jeshua or Joshua ben Jozadek (Jehozadak), the first high priest of the restored temple and one of its rebuilders. There is evidence in Lev. 4:3, 5 and 16 for the practice of anointing the high priest. The title here translated 'prince' is applied to the high priest Onias III in Dan. 11:22. The most likely contender is Jeshua. The date would suit all three, i.e., 538 B.C.E., and this fits in neatly with the seven weeks of years (forty-nine years).

> 2. Sixty-two weeks, i.e., 434 years, from the rebuilding of Jerusalem to the demise of 'an anointed one' (v. 26) and the despoiling of the city and sanctuary by 'the people [troops] of the prince who is to come'.

There is one further piece of information in the text (v. 27) which helps to determine the date of the end of this period, namely, that 'the prince who is to come' will 'make a strong covenant [pact] with many for one week . . .'. The resolution of the problem of the sixty-two weeks, however, is dependent on the delineation of the third period, the one week (seven years).

> 3. One week, i.e., seven years, from the death of the 'anointed one' (v. 26) to the end of the half-week (second half) during which sacrifice and offering is to be proscribed (v. 27).

With the accession of Antiochus IV in 175 B.C.E. the Seleucid attitude towards the Jewish community altered dramatically. The latter became caught up in the new policy of enforced Hellenisation. What developed was a situation in which Jewish Hellenisers found themselves in positions of great influence. One of these named Jason (Joshua in Hebrew) was able, through bribery, to oust his brother Onias III from the high priesthood. Some three years later Jason himself fell victim to the machinations of his compatriot Menelaus. In his effort to comply with the terms of the proffered bribe, Menelaus resorted to use of the temple gold, an action resolutely opposed by the former high priest Onias. By stealthy means Onias was induced to leave the safety of his hiding place and was summarily put to death. That was in 171 B.C.E. Four years later, as part of the policy of the Seleucid regime and as a direct result of uprisings in Jerusalem, Jewish religious practices were proscribed. In addition, the hated Akra was constructed and the temple defiled. What occurred during this seven-year period and, in particular, during the second 'half of the week' is succinctly described in v. 27. The final week of years is therefore the period from 171 to 164 B.C.E.

So far as the reinterpreted Jeremianic prophecy is concerned, there are two clearly fixed points, namely, 587-538 B.C.E. and 171-164 B.C.E. The accuracy of the first seven-week period and of the closing single week is thereby attested. The intervening period, the sixty-two weeks, however, may not be so readily dealt with. Precise reckoning would require a figure of 434 years, but only 367 of these can be accounted for, i.e., from 538 to 171 B.C.E. One explanation is that this lengthy period, designed to accommodate a certain fixed schema, served merely to join together the two periods in which the Jewish author had particular interest, that of the Exile which was the focal point of the original prophecy and that of his people's situation under Antiochus IV.

It was not the purpose of the author of the book of Daniel to present his readers with a textbook on history. It was his express purpose, however, to focus on those events which had determined the course of his people's life, and to show how, with the aid of a selected prophecy, this flow of events might still be seen to fall within the control of a God who had not left his people without hope. This is a viewpoint to which both Judaism and Christianity have clung with great tenacity. For the former, at least from the evidence of the writings that span the two eras, there will be a time of great conflict, followed by the judgment and destruction of the hostile powers. The Holy City of Jerusalem will be restored and God will take his rightful place as the Ruler of the world. Various groups within Judaism and those on the periphery, such as the Qumran sectaries, may have expressed these matters in different ways, but the essential elements appear in one form or another. (See further E. Schürer, *The History of the Jewish People in the Age of Jesus Christ (175 B.C. – A.D. 135)*, 2, rev. ed. 514-54.)

So far as eschatological hope is concerned, Christian doctrine has followed a different course from the one briefly alluded to. New Testament writers, sometimes guided closely by their interpretation of the book of Daniel, in particular 7:13-14 and 9:24-27, found the fulfilment of this hope in the person of Jesus Christ. In Luke 1:8-25 the angel Gabriel, the guardian and mentor of Daniel, appears to Zechariah. It is this same angel who announces to Mary that she will give birth to a son whose kingdom will be everlasting (Luke 1:33).

Both Judaism and Christianity, faiths spawned by the ancient Hebrew Scriptures, acknowledge that there is one God and one alone, and he is the Lord of history. Each has its part to play in the unfolding of the divine purpose. In this respect, what E. Bloch has called the 'third Testament' (Romans 9–11) is of special significance.

Some details in vv. 25-27 require fuller treatment. The translation 'with squares and moat' (v. 25) makes little sense as a description of the city of Jerusalem. It is best taken as an expression suggesting completeness. The text of vv. 26-27 contains some difficulties. The MT of v. 26b has Antiochus as the subject — 'his end shall come with a flood . . .' — whereas the RSV translation and some commentators relate these words to the fate of the city. As a general description of the predicament of the faithful, with its reference to war and desolations, v. 26b has a fair measure of accuracy if so applied. It makes more sense as a reference to the city than to Antiochus. Many efforts have been made to explain the enigmatic 'upon the wing of abominations' (v. 27). The general sense is that the one who is the enemy of the faithful, the 'desolator' of God's people and sanctuary, will sweep to victory through his abominations, but it will be a limited victory only. There will come a time, at the end of the second half-week according to the author, when the destroyer himself will be destroyed.

These themes are taken up again in ch. 11. The profanation of the temple is the subject of 11:31 where the words 'abomination' and 'desolate' occur. The Hebrew text contains a play on words. The Canaanite pantheon included a Baal Shamem, the god of heaven. The author of Daniel recalls this particular aspect of early idolatry by occasional use of terms such as *meshomem* (9:27; 11:31) and *shomem* (9:27; 12:11). What he is pointing out is that Antiochus has introduced nothing new. The nation has faced before those who sought to subvert its worship of the one true God, those who would endeavour to supplant the God of creation with a god of human devising. At times the details of Daniel's presentation may be the victim of textual difficulty, and the meaning partially obscured, but the impact of the message is clear beyond doubt. If this message is handled unwisely and allowed to become the tool of crude speculation, it leads inevitably to absurdity. But when it is recognized as the persistent proclamation of the God of Israel as the Lord of history, it is a strengthening word — not to one past generation only, but to the faithful of all generations.

Modern proclamation may adopt different forms and use different methods, but if it ceases to set forth what the book of Daniel here expounds, it will cease to declare the full measure of the Word of God.

CHAPTER 10

DANIEL'S COMMISSION
Daniel 10:1-21

Chapter 10 or, more accurately, the section 10:1 – 11:1, constitutes an introduction to what is, in the main, one long, detailed revelation that brings the book to its climax. This in turn is followed by:

(i) a recital of historical events, 11:2-39, giving meagre information on the first, second, and third kingdoms and concentrating on the fourth (cf. 2:40-45; 7:17-26; 8:9-14, 22-26),

(ii) a prediction concerning the 'end time', 11:40 – 12:3(4), and

(iii) a conclusion, 12:5-13.

Chapter 10 contains more material of a personal nature on the central figure of Daniel than is to be found outside the stories of chs. 1 – 6. We are allowed to see a little more than the erstwhile unquestioning, obedient recipient of visions. What we have in this chapter is reminiscent of the prophetic 'call' or 'commissioning' narratives. In this case it would be inaccurate to speak of an initial 'call'. Rather, there is here something akin to an authenticating act on the part of the deity, prior to the seer's receiving a revelation of considerable scope and significance. On Daniel's part there is a reluctance to accept the commission, and signs of an attempted evasion of responsibility, recalling the reactions of other great Hebrew heroes, notably Moses, Isaiah, and Jeremiah. After repeated reassurances (vv. 11, 12, 16, and 19) he regains his composure. His full recovery from the shock of the main vision (vv. 5-7) has been slow and painful. The author takes care to point out that Daniel is not greater than the prophets of past days; he is no more willing than Moses, no more certain of his own worthiness than Isaiah, and no less apprehensive than Jer-

119

emiah. Yet it is to him, of all people, that the great and final revelation is to be made. It is given to Daniel to know the secrets that have been hidden from all others.

1   The superscription to this chapter contains a number of interesting points. This, the most extensive of Daniel's vision-interpretation experiences, is dated 'in the third year of Cyrus king of Persia' and is therefore quite unmistakably the final contribution from the ostensibly sixth-century hero. We are informed in 1:21 that 'Daniel continued until the first year of King Cyrus'. The texts are not contradictory. What 1:21 does is no more than record that Daniel lived to see the advent of Cyrus and therefore the fall of Babylon and the opportunity to return to the Promised Land. The description of Cyrus as 'king of Persia' is unusual and suggests a practice, current in Hellenistic times, according to which Cyrus was identified in terms of his origins rather than his exploits. For the first and only time in the second section of the book (chs. 7 – 12) Daniel is also referred to by his Babylonian name, Belteshazzar. It will be recalled that this was given to him by 'the chief of the eunuchs' during the period of his schooling (1:7). This should be seen in conjunction with the use of the third person, a feature common to chs. 1 – 6, but which occurs previously in this second section only at the commencement of ch. 7. These two departures from the normal format of chs. 7 – 12 suggest something of particular importance in this chapter. Not only is the hero of the early stories here clearly identified as the seer of the visionary experiences, but Daniel is authenticated as a man of God's calling, whose word is steadfast and sure. This is brought out more clearly in the treatment of v. 9. Just as the word that he received was trustworthy, so, too, was his understanding of it. But one rather odd statement remains to be dealt with: 'And the word was true, and it was a great conflict'. If the RSV translation is retained, the word 'conflict' could be taken as a reference to the angelic princely struggle mentioned in vv. 13 and 20-21. The Hebrew word *tsaba* does not allow the suggestion that a personal inner conflict is being spoken of, a construction that could be placed on the RSV rendering. Ibn Ezra saw here a reference to the angelic host, a not uncommon use of the Hebrew word, whereas Rashi took the word to signify not conflict, or warfare, or heavenly beings, but a period of time. Consequently, he translated the expression eschatologically. The word, i.e., the revelation vouchsafed to Daniel, was true, but it was for the distant future.

2-4 With v. 2 the text moves to the first person, and this is retained throughout the remainder of the book. The reason for Daniel's mourning is not given. It may have been induced by distress over current events or it could have been preparatory to the receiving of a revelation. The latter suits the context admirably. Verse 12 may be cited in support of this, and there is evidence of a similar purpose in Ezra 8:21 and 2(4) Esdr. 5:19-22. Whatever its reason, the lengthy mourning, or fast, does not appear to have followed the customary lines (cf. 2 Sam. 12:20 and 14:2). That it was not a complete fast seems to be indicated by the singling out of the rather patrician items from which Daniel abstained.

Verse 4 introduces an interesting note so far as the liturgical calendar is concerned. It was on the 'twenty-fourth day of the first month' that Daniel experienced the vision. Presumably that coincided with the conclusion of the twenty-one-day fast. In other words, he had fasted, at least partially, from the third to the twenty-fourth day of the month of Nisan, as it was called in postexilic times. If this reckoning is correct, Daniel's period of 'mourning' must have included Passover. That a hero of the faith might have failed to partake of the traditional four cups of wine and the unleavened bread created a real difficulty for some earlier Jewish commentators. Ibn Ezra was one of these, and the solution he proposed was to relate the first month of v. 4, not to the calendar year, but to the anniversary of Cyrus's accession to the throne of Babylon. This explanation may be incorrect, but it does indicate how seriously the great festival occasions were taken.

In 8:2 Daniel was transported in his vision to the banks of the river Ulai (so the RSV and most commentators). Here again he is by a river — this time one of the most notable of all, the Tigris. But he is not there only in vision; he is there physically and, as v. 7 indicates, with friends.

5-9 A comparison of the description of 'the man' of vv. 5 and 6 with that of the figure who appears in Rev. 1:13-16 is both interesting and informative, particularly in the light of the temptation to identify the two, which appealed to earlier Christian commentators. The Danielic figure was 'a man' (or to give full force to the Hebrew numeral which is used, 'a single man', 'a lone man'); he was 'clothed in linen'; his loins were 'girded with the gold of Uphaz', i.e., there was a large beltlike garment around him; his body 'was like beryl'; his face was 'like the appearance of lightning'; his eyes were 'like flaming torches'; his arms and legs were 'like the gleam of burnished bronze'; and finally, 'the sound of his words [was] like the noise of a multitude'.

The 'son of man' of Rev. 1:13-16 has only three features in common with these, plus three additional features that bear no relationship. In a sense there is a general sameness about the two and, given the purpose of each description, this is hardly surprising, for the author of the book of Revelation throughout his work draws heavily on the language and imagery of the book of Daniel. The 'remarkable similarities' between the two figures are not really as remarkable as Di Lella (*Daniel*, 279) suggests. It is not valid to move beyond this to an identification of the two. Much of the imagery of Dan. 10:5-6 is drawn from the book of Ezekiel where the description is either of a messenger (Ezek. 9:2-3, 11) or of a cherub (Ezek. 1:5-28).

There is in the 'call narratives', from Isaiah 6 to Ezekiel 1 to Daniel 10, an intensifying of the numinous. This is accomplished by means of more direct association with the human form, but with the introduction of strikingly vivid, almost grotesque apparel, and the addition of a booming, frightening voice. Some preparation for this last-mentioned feature is to be found in Ezek 1:25. By this means a tradition was established. In the future, no ethereal figure may be presented in ways which do not, to some degree at least, correspond with it. It is one thing, however, to recognize the creation of a pattern; it is quite another to discern a theological nexus.

It should be pointed out that the apparition of vv. 5 and 6 is not to be identified with the angel Gabriel. If the latter does make an appearance in this chapter, it is not until v. 10. What we have in these verses is something far more awesome than a mere angelic being. Moreover, Gabriel has appeared to Daniel previously without any such overpowering effect as that described in vv. 8-9. Nor is there any evidence to suggest that an identification with the angel Michael is any less wide of the mark.

This is not an instance of one or the other of two more or less ordinary angelic creatures being endowed with grotesque and frightening features. The subject of these verses stands on its own; it is quite independent of any other in the book. This should not be surprising, for there are many elements in the book of Daniel that lack parallels, not least the fourth man in the fiery furnace (3:25). The desire to align these various figures, the one with the other, betrays the influence of a traditional exegesis which did so for apologetic and dogmatic reasons.

Though v. 6 mentions a voice with 'words like the noise of a multitude', there is no definite indication in the text of any ordinary communication with Daniel. Verse 9 speaks only of the effect of the sound of the words, i.e., they were audible but, because of their great noise, not comprehensible. If this is so, then it is the very figure itself that is the revelation, and it is in the reaction of Daniel that there is evidence of a message received. This revelation, seen only by Daniel, is the guarantee of the presence of the glory and power of God. Its immediate effect on him was overpowering: his strength departed from him; the colour drained from his face; and he was left emaciated and helpless (v. 8). There is a reminder here of the statement in Exod. 33:20 to the effect that one cannot see the face of God and live. That Daniel survives is helpful in the identification of the figure. In this strange way Daniel has been made to feel as though he has come close to seeing God. It is a theophany-like experience, but it has been contrived by the author for a particular purpose, and the author may have been more than slightly amused had he been aware of the later attempts to identify his imaginary figure. Of much greater importance is what happened to Daniel. The immediate effect was to leave him in an inert state, his life-force almost spent. The description of this is painstakingly graphic, underlining its importance. Moreover, at various points throughout the chapter he is shown struggling to regain his composure (vv. 11, 16, 17).

The enormity of this bizarre event is further emphasized by the description of the behaviour of Daniel's companions. Though they had witnessed nothing, perhaps not even heard anything, they were gripped by fear and fled frantically to find a hiding-place (v. 7). Attention is often drawn to the experience recorded in Acts 9:7, but the parallel is not a close one.

The importance of Daniel's revelatory experience is not to be seen in any supposed light that it might throw on the identity of the enigmatic figures that appear from time to time in the book of Daniel. If that is an issue at all it is a peripheral one, and serves only to distract attention from the more important matter. The importance lies in the authenticating nature of this experience. Its likeness to Isaiah 6 and Ezekiel 1 suggests that it is in fact an authentication of Daniel's call. His words (and extremely significant ones are to follow) may be readily accepted, for both he and they have on them the unmistakable imprimatur of God. What later authors might make of Daniel's experience is one thing; what his immediate readers were to see in it was quite another. It is not by accident that on this occasion Daniel should be accompanied by others (v. 7) not privy to what Daniel was permitted to see, but witness nevertheless to his chosen purpose.

If it is asked why such an authentication stands here and not earlier in the book, the answer must be found in the nature of the long, detailed final revelation which is to follow. Most of this is presented as a description of historical events which find their culmination in the fall of Antiochus Epiphanes. For it to be accepted requires an unequivocal sign from God, such as that now given directly to Daniel, and indirectly to those who accompanied him. But the historical résumé is not the only forthcoming word; there is also the clearest note of hope yet to be made, that even death itself will yield up its victims (12:2). That alone would require the authenticating seal of God.

10-14 'And behold, a hand touched me . . .' (v. 10). To whom did the hand belong? The most likely answer, despite Di Lella's assertion to the contrary (*Daniel*, 281), is that the hand did not belong to the visionary figure depicted in vv. 5 and 6. If not to that one, then to whom else? It is a comforting hand, accompanied by reassuring words (v. 11), and the one who normally fulfils such a role in these chapters is the angel Gabriel. In chs. 8 and 9 Gabriel is closely associated with the seer, and there is no reason to suppose that the guardian angel changed his identity at this stage. The first act on his part is to touch Daniel (see also vv. 16 and 18) and to set him on his hands and knees. The recovery from the awesome experience of vv. 5-9 is, for Daniel, a slow and measured process. The word of assurance is twofold.

Daniel is again addressed as a 'man greatly beloved' (see 9:23). The confirmation of this, as in the previous chapter, is in the words, the revelation, that the angelic messenger brings. Daniel regains some of his strength and stands upright though trembling. It is this sign of a continuing frightened state that elicits from Gabriel the further comforting word, 'Fear not. . .', followed by the assurance that Daniel's preparation for this moment, by fasting and prayer, has not gone unnoticed (v. 12). Indeed, from the very outset of this ascetic exercise, the purpose of which is now clear, his words have been heard. The parallel with the role of Gabriel in 9:20-23 is clear beyond doubt, and strongly suggests that he has been correctly identified at this point in the chapter. Gabriel's presence is one sure sign of God's response. The frightening experience of vv. 5-9 was an interlude, a very necessary one, but now Daniel is once more in the hands of his guardian and tutor.

The reason for the delay in Gabriel's response to Daniel is given in v. 13, and it brings to the fore a feature that is to become more prominent as the book progresses, namely, the combative action of the angels on behalf of the nation. Gabriel himself has been engaged in such action with 'the prince of the kingdom of Persia'. This had continued throughout the twenty-one days of Daniel's 'mourning' (v. 2) and, as events will show, is still far from completion. In Gabriel's absence the battle was taken up by Michael. What is clear is that the expression 'the prince of the kingdom of Persia' does not mean the earthly Persian monarch. The allusion here, and in v. 20, is to a cosmic battle being fought between extraterrestrial forces. This is an important feature of the power struggle depicted in the book of Daniel and in later apocalyptic literature. The fortunes of the earthly powers are determined by the outcome of a combat that rages in the heavens. The Dead Sea Scrolls describe a war which 'symbolizes the eternal struggle between the spirits of Light and Darkness' (G. Vermes, *The Dead Sea Scrolls in English*, 123-24). In the NT Apocalypse the protagonists are 'Michael and his angels' on the one side, and 'the dragon and his angels' on the other (Rev. 12:7). The dragon is identified in the succeeding verses as 'that ancient serpent, who is called the Devil and Satan, the deceiver of the whole world' (Rev. 12:9). This suggests a development considerably beyond the mere clash of the nations as in the book of

Daniel. The latter is singularly lacking in anything that might be construed as demonology. Angelology is there, in quite a developed form, but its counterpart is not to be found. The enemies of Gabriel and Michael are simply referred to as 'princes' (*sarim* in Hebrew), a term which may also be applied to the champions of Israel. Michael is one of the chief *sarim* (v. 13) and appears also in 1 Enoch 20:1-8 as one of the seven archangels of Jewish faith. He features many times in 1 Enoch, as do Gabriel, Uriel, Raphael, Raguel, and Remiel (1 Enoch 9:1; 10:11; 41:9; 54:6; 68:2; 71:3ff.).

That Israel had its own angelic patron is found for the first time in Dan. 8:15-16, and again in 12:1. Michael is presented as the nation's champion, 'Michael, the great prince who has charge of your people'. The inference to be drawn from 10:13 and 10:20 is that Persia and Greece also have their patron angels. Some scholars have found the earliest biblical reference, an oblique one admittedly, to such a concept in Deut. 32:8. The MT of this verse provides little support for this, but the LXX, with its 'sons of Israel', could be pressed into service, the more so in light of the reconstruction put on it in Qumran's 4QDeut. Other earlier biblical texts used to support the notion of angelic or celestial champions are Deut. 4:19; Josh. 24:15; Judg. 5:19-21; Isa. 24:21; and Psalm 82. This material is far from persuasive. Among the postbiblical texts that give a much clearer picture are 1 Enoch 89:51ff.; 90:20ff.; and Jubilees 15. It has been claimed that in origin those beings are derived from the 'dispossessed gods' (Bertholet), or are a remnant of polytheism (Di Lella). Parallels have been noted with the shepherd-ruler-gods of classical Greece. If the origin of the concept is far from clear, so, too, is the reason for its appearance. One possible reason is that in time it became necessary to account for the vagaries of God's dealings with his people, i.e., the blame had to be placed somewhere other than on the deity himself. A growing appreciation of the transcendence of God might also have been a contributing factor. In other words, some intermediate stage of existence not only bridged the gap, but maintained it.

The interest of the chapter reverts to the fortunes of the people of Israel 'in the latter days' (v. 14). The revelation to Daniel so far is in part only; there is still 'vision' concerning the end. The closing statement in v. 14 is sufficiently close to the wording and the sense of Hab. 2:3a to suggest that the author had that text in mind. This possibility is strengthened when it is recalled that a similar use of the verse is made by the Qumran sectaries. The commentary on Hab. 2:31 reads:

> Interpreted, this means that the final age shall be pro-longed, and shall exceed all that the Prophets have said; for the mysteries of God are outstanding. (Translation by G. Vermes, *The Dead Sea Scrolls*, 239)

There is here both agreement and disagreement with the author of Daniel. Whereas the latter wrote in keen expectation of the end, the Qumran commentator, writing somewhat later and in changed circumstances, indicates that the last days will be drawn out. Where they agree is in their acceptance that it is legitimate exegesis to go beyond the plain meaning of the prophets (see Dan. 9:24ff.), 'for the mysteries of God are outstanding'.

15-21(11:1)   Daniel's recovery (v. 11) is only partial; again he is overcome by the strain of the experience. It may well be that his discomfort has been increased by the announcement that fur-ther, and particularly significant revelation, is to follow (v. 14). Instead of an eagerness to be caught up in the council of the divine, instead of an ardent desire to be made aware of what is about to happen, one finds a reluctance on Daniel's part which surpasses that of Isaiah and Jeremiah. Speech failed him. Only after his lips have been touched by 'one in the likeness of the sons of men' (Gabriel) is he able to offer any reply and, even then, it is the faltering confession that he is unable to proceed. With no strength, no breath, how can he possibly engage Gabriel in conversation (v. 17)!

There is no reason to suppose that another angelic being makes an appearance at v. 16. If the words 'one in the likeness of the sons of men' are taken to signal the entrance of another interlo-cutor at this point, why not draw a similar conclusion from the presence of the words 'one having the appearance of a man' in v. 18? It is the necessary indirect style that creates the problem, rather than the actual content of the verses. There is one angelic speaker, and one only, in ch. 10, and he is the one who comes to Daniel's aid in v. 10, who provides the helping hand that touches the seer three times (vv. 10, 16, 18), and who reassuringly sets him on his feet and prepares him for new revelation. The vision-figure of vv. 5 and 6 does not communicate. Its words do not contain a message; if anything, they add to Daniel's fear and confusion.

The pattern established in vv. 10-11 and 15-16 is continued in vv. 18 and 19. The words of assurance, though repetitive in part ('O . . . man greatly beloved' [cf. v. 11] and 'Fear not' [cf. v. 12]), provide an added emphasis. By the formula 'peace be with you', clearly not the familiar greeting because of its position in mid-sentence, Daniel is assured that all will be well, and that the strength that has momentarily departed from him will return. These words have their desired effect (v. 19b), and Daniel stands ready to hear what it is that constitutes 'the vision . . . for days yet to come' (v. 14). Step by step, perhaps rather laboriously, the author has prepared his readers for an announcement of great moment. The hapless, though greatly privileged Daniel has been made to stumble his way towards the finale.

The question in v. 20 makes little sense unless it is taken as rhetorical. There is an awkwardness in the ordering of the statements which follow that has led to a number of attempted re-arrangements. However, the sense is clear. Gabriel announces that he is about to return to the confrontation with 'the prince of Persia' (see v. 13), and once he has been defeated, the challenge of 'the prince of Greece' will be dealt with. Again, Michael is singled out as the champion of Israel ('your prince', v. 21) and Gabriel's companion in battle. These words are fully comprehensible only in the light of what is to come in chs. 11 and 12.

'But I will tell you what is inscribed in the book of truth' (v. 21a) appears to be related to 11:2a, 'And now I will show you the truth'. If this is so, we need not speculate further on the nature of this book. We are not dealing with a reference to the prophetic writings, nor is there here anything more than the most superficial of connections with 'the books' of 7:10. What is alluded to is the record of what is about to happen. It is the purpose of the author to suggest that what will occur in the future, up to and including the time of the end, is so firmly fixed that it has already received written form. History will proceed according to this script. The Hebrew expression employed in v. 21a indicates a firm or reliable writing rather than a 'book of truth', and it is going far beyond the evidence to speak of 'the book of Truth' as does Lacocque (*Daniel*, 210).

CHAPTER 11

THE PROFANER OF THE TEMPLE
Daniel 11:1-45

---

1 The significance of 'And as for me, in the first year of Darius the Mede . . .' is not at all clear. What is clear, however, is that the words which immediately follow should be attached to 10:21. Gabriel's support is not for Darius the Mede, but for his fellow angelic cohort, Michael. The words in question are usually declared to be a gloss, intended as an introduction to what a later editor understood as a distinctly separate vision. The formula 'in the Nth year of so-and-so' forms part of a superscription which is to be found in a number of places throughout the book (1:1; 2:1; 7:1; 8:1; 9:1; 10:1). It thus afforded an ideal point, when appropriate, for a chapter division. (For a note on the often arbitrary nature of chapter divisions and their late imposition on the text, see under 4:1-3.)

2 (539-331 B.C.E.). What has been firmly fixed by God in the annals of the nations is about to be revealed to Daniel. The verse may be taken to suggest a total of either four or five Persian monarchs. The passage could refer to four kings in addition to Cyrus, or he could be included in the four. All in all, eleven Persian kings reigned during this period. Though nine of these receive mention in various parts of the Hebrew Scriptures, the practice appears to have developed, when certain listings were required, to allow the part to stand for the whole (Ezra 4:5-7; Dan. 7:6). If four kings are intended by the text, and that is the more likely, those in addition to Cyrus would be either the next three in line, or three of the following significant monarchs, Darius I (522-486), Xerxes I (486-465), Artaxerxes I (465-424), or Darius II (433-404). The mention of strength, riches, and ani-

129

mosity towards Greece could be a general and all-inclusive note rather than a reference to one particular monarch. Beyond that is the area of mere speculation.

3-4 (331-323 B.C.E.). There is little doubt that the subject of v. 3 is Alexander the Great (see 8:5-8, 21). At the peak of his career, and after staggering successes that allowed him to extend his domain to the river Indus, Alexander died in Babylon at the age of 33. One by one his possible successors, a half-brother and two sons, one born posthumously and the other illegitimate, were put out of the way. The vast empire which Alexander had so expeditiously created, fell into the hands of his generals, and was in fact 'divided toward the four winds of heaven'. The various factions which developed immediately after his death occupied themselves for some time with claim and counterclaim, intrigue and counter-intrigue, with not a few pitched battles resulting from all these machinations. The most significant of these was fought near Gaza in 312 B.C.E. As an outcome of this battle in particular, two centres of power were established. Over the next century and a half, the course of events in this part of the ancient Near East was determined by the struggle for overall dominance. First one was to be in the ascendancy, and then the other.

5-6 (323-246 B.C.E.). By 323 B.C.E. Ptolemy I Soter had established himself securely in Egypt, though the title of king was not assumed until 305 B.C.E. It is he, then, who is the first 'king of the south' (v. 5). His ally at the Battle of Gaza was the former satrap of Babylon, Seleucus. A little earlier he had been forced to flee to Ptolemy in Egypt for protection from the forces of Antigonus. The Gaza victory enabled him to return north. In 301 Seleucus gained a further victory at Ipsus, this time without the participation of Ptolemy, who had taken the opportunity to consolidate his control over Palestine. Despite the actions of his erstwhile ally, Seleucus I Nicator emerged in these years as the greater of the two so far as territorial regions were concerned, and well merited the judgment of v. 5. His son Antiochus I Soter (281-261) is the sole monarch of the two regimes not to receive mention in this chapter.

The alliance alluded to in v. 6 came about during the reigns of Ptolemy II Philadelphus (285-246) of Egypt and Antiochus II

Theos (261-246) of the Seleucid empire. Ptolemy proved himself to be an extraordinarily capable administrator and exploited to the full the lands under his control. He had twice been involved in war with the northern kingdom, but in the year 253 B.C.E. decided that a marriage alliance between the two houses was in his own interests. Antiochus was persuaded to set aside his half-sister wife Laodice in favour of Berenice, the daughter of Ptolemy. The arrangement displaced the sons of Laodice and provided for Berenice's son to succeed to the throne. In 246, however, Ptolemy was killed and, with this threat removed, Antiochus nominated the eldest of Laodice's sons as his own successor. Though Berenice had been discarded by the king, Laodice made sure of her own position by arranging not only the poisoning of the king but also the murder of Berenice, her infant son, and a number of her Egyptian attendants (v. 6).

It is beyond the purpose of the book of Daniel to include references to all the important events of the time. Its interests are dictated by its own approach. One occurrence, however, should not be allowed to go unmentioned. That was the translation of the Hebrew Torah into Greek. From the point of view of the development of Judaism within the diaspora, this may have been the most significant happening of all. Ptolemy II lent his support to the project, not for religious reasons, but for political. He saw it as a means of serving the needs of his Jewish mercenaries as well as those of the sizeable Jewish community in Alexandria.

7-9 (246-223 B.C.E.). The sequel to the assassinations within the Antiochene royal household is found in v. 7. The 'branch' referred to here was Ptolemy III Euergetes (246-221), the brother of Berenice. His victorious northward march took him into the city of Antioch itself and most likely as far as Babylon. News of disturbances in Egypt prevented his following up these successes and he was forced to return, but not without the spoils of war in the form of objects mentioned in v. 8. Brief reference is made in v. 9 to the incursion of the army of Seleucus II Callinicus into Egypt in 242 B.C.E. What success he had was short-lived and he quickly retired north.

10-19 (223-187 B.C.E.). One of the 'sons' of v. 10 was Seleucus III Soter (226-223), but by far the more important, and the principal subject of this section, was Antiochus III the Great (223-187). Since the rise of the Seleucid and Ptolemaic states, southern Syria (Coele-Syria) and Palestine, and therefore the area including Judea, had been in the hands of the 'king of the south'. This position was to change during the reign of Antiochus III. Shortly after the death of Ptolemy III in 221 and the succession of his young son Ptolemy IV, Antiochus was able to regain Seleucia, the port of Antioch, and began to lay claim to the land immediately south of his. What is known as the Fourth Syrian War broke out in 219 B.C.E. with early victories going to Antiochus (v. 10), largely because of important defections from the Ptolemaic ranks. The immediate Seleucid advance, however, was only temporary. At Raphia, in June 217, Antiochus suffered a crushing defeat, and was fortunate to be able to return safely to Antioch, and even more fortunate to be able to come to an agreement with his victor. Ptolemy, whose behaviour tended towards the unstable, failed to follow up his advantage beyond occupying certain areas that had previously been lost. Daniel 11:12 is a terse comment on his arrogant and erratic behaviour.

Ironically, the new-found strength of the Egyptian army provided one of the chief problems Ptolemy had to face on his return. It was the local Egyptians among his troops, rather than the mercenaries, who had given him victory at Raphia, and so the local populace began to assert their national claims. In 205 Ptolemy IV Philopator died under mysterious circumstances and was succeeded by his five-year-old son, Ptolemy V Epiphanes (203-181 B.C.E.). This was an opportune time for Antiochus III to embark once more on his ambitious plans for expansion. He entered into a pact with Philip V of Macedon, thus safeguarding his northwestern front, and proceeded to push south through Palestine. The arrival of winter curtailed his southward advance, and this gave the Egyptian forces under Scopas time to assert themselves. In 199 B.C.E. the two armies faced each other at Paneion, near present-day Banias, the ancient Caesarea Philippi, at the headwaters of the river Jordan. Victory went to Antiochus, and from that date Palestine (including Judea) came under the sway of the Seleucids (vv. 13ff.).

Verse 14 is of particular importance, for it betrays the stance of the author. Throughout the century-long strife the small Jewish population had been afflicted by one set of invaders after

another, and many Jews had either been taken to Egypt or had
become mercenaries in the Ptolemaic armies. With the increase
of the influence of Antiochus III a pro-Seleucid party arose in
Jerusalem, the leaders of which were the powerful and influential
Tobiad family and the high priest, Simon II 'the Just'. This division within the Jewish population was very much in evidence
at the time when the book of Daniel received its extant form.
Within the comparatively small community, sides were being
taken, factions formed, and cleavages created. These were greatly
to affect the course of Jewish history over the next fifty years or
more. To some extent, the two sides are represented by the author
of Daniel on the one hand, and the author of Ecclesiasticus on
the other. The latter includes Simon the Just among the famous
men worthy of praise (Ecclus. 50:1ff.), a judgment that would
not have met with the approval of the former. For his part, the
author of Daniel could not forget that Antiochus III was the
father of the hated persecutor, Antiochus IV Epiphanes.

The account of the continuing conflict between Antiochus III
and the Ptolemaic general Scopas is resumed at v. 15. After his
defeat at Paneion, Scopas took refuge with his remaining troops
in the coastal fortress of Sidon, but was forced to surrender the
following year. The city of Jerusalem itself was partly destroyed
during this struggle, and eventually a new master stood un-
opposed 'in the glorious land' (v. 16). (For this expression see
8:9.) By and large the change in overlordship did not affect the
Jewish people adversely, and there were indications that Antiochus, at least initially, went to some trouble to win the support
of his new subjects.

Antiochus did not capitalise on his successes by invading Egypt,
but did add several of the coastal cities of Asia Minor to his list
of conquests. A peace treaty was drawn up with Ptolemy V who
had been crowned in 197 B.C.E. and, as a seal to the alliance,
Cleopatra, the daughter of Antiochus, was given in marriage to
the young southern monarch. By this means Antiochus had hoped
to undermine the strength of his rival, but contrary to this design,
Cleopatra remained politically loyal to her husband (v. 17).

The subsequent actions of Antiochus proved to be his undoing.
In moving into 'the coastlands' of Asia Minor (v. 18), and even
further westward into Thrace, he seriously underestimated the
determination and the power of Rome. This error of judgment

was to cost him dearly. At the Battle of Magnesia in 190 B.C.E. the Seleucid forces were routed by a Roman army under the command of one of the two famous Scipio brothers (v. 18). As a result of this defeat Antiochus was obliged to pay heavy tribute from a treasury that had already been seriously depleted by the relatively generous, though politically motivated, taxation measures. One further source of revenue that lay open to the impecunious king was the temple riches of the many sanctuaries throughout his scattered empire. While he was engaged in one such plundering exercise he met an ignominious death at the hands of the outraged local citizens. That was at Elymais in 187 B.C.E. (v. 19).

Antiochus III had been a ruler of considerable achievement and renown. He had accomplished what previous members of his dynasty had failed to do; he had conquered Coele-Syria and Palestine. But in enticing the Romans, through a political miscalculation, to set foot on the continent of Asia he had created momentous problems for his successors. One of these, later to take the throne as Antiochus IV, served an apprenticeship as an honoured hostage of Rome. With a foothold on Asian soil, the army of Rome opened up new possibilities. The balance of power was already altering, and it is more than ironic that the reform party in Jerusalem should be gearing itself for cooperation with the Seleucids at a time when the fortunes of the latter were beginning to ebb.

20-39 (187-167 B.C.E.). The number of verses given to this period is a clear indication of where the author's interest and concern lay. The immediate successor to Antiochus III was his son, Seleucus IV Philopator. Of such little consequence was he that the author of Daniel is able to dismiss him in one verse (v. 20). The burden of making heavy payments to Rome passed from royal father to royal son, and the reference in this difficultly worded text is possibly to one particular effort that Seleucus IV made to augment his income. It is known that he dispatched his official, Heliodorus, to pillage the treasury of the Jerusalem temple, an episode that is related quite graphically in 2 Macc. 3:1-40. It proved to be an abortive mission, for entering the treasury Heliodorus was confronted by a terrifying apparition, and escaped with his life only through the good offices of the high priest.

So the story was told. Heliodorus himself was an extremely ambitious man, and may have had pretensions to the throne, but in these pretensions, and in the skill to give them effect, he was more than matched by the erstwhile prisoner of Rome, Antiochus, for it was he who engineered the assassination of Seleucus in 175 B.C.E.

The author's arch villain has thus reached centre stage, and is to occupy that position throughout the remainder of this chapter. It is Antiochus who is the 'contemptible person' of v. 21, the 'sinful root' of 1 Macc. 1:10, and the 'arrogant and terrible man' of 4 Macc. 4:15. The rightful heir to the Seleucid throne had been Demetrius, elder son of Antiochus III, but for some inexplicable reason he had been exchanged for Antiochus IV as the royal hostage in Rome. This left the younger son, also named Antiochus, who seemingly had two protectors, the rivals Heliodorus and Antiochus IV. The latter had a great propensity for picking up useful friends along the way, and not the least of these was the king of Pergamum, who placed his troops at the disposal of the uncle of the legitimate claimant. That Antiochus managed to ingratiate himself with the citizens of Athens on his homeward journey is further evidence of the cunning referred to in 8:23 (see comments).

The armies spoken of in v. 22 must be those of his Seleucid rivals, while the 'prince of the covenant' could be one of three persons: Demetrius the rightful king, Ptolemy VI with whom an alliance (covenant) had been made earlier, or the high priest Onias III. The likelihood is that it is the last mentioned, for it is known that Onias strongly opposed the policies of Antiochus IV. An account in 2 Macc. 4:7-10 describes how Jason, the brother of Onias, was able to bribe the king and so gain for himself the powerful office of high priest. A little later Jason was 'hoist with his own petard' by the even more unscrupulous Menelaus, who is described as 'possessing no qualification for the high priesthood, but having the hot temper of a cruel tyrant and the rage of a savage wild beast' (2 Macc. 4:25), a fitting ally for Antiochus IV. Jason, though vanquished, emerges again in relation to the events described in v. 28.

There had been for some time a pro-Seleucid party in Jerusalem drawn mainly from the influential families, and adopting this particular stance for both political and religious reasons. It is to this section of Jerusalem's citizenry that v. 23 refers. The same verse suggests that, while Antiochus was a formidable and dangerous foe, he was also a shiftless and unreliable friend. The region had become used to the plundering tactics of monarchs over the years, but Antiochus had the ability to outshine all of his predecessors in this as well as in other nefarious practices. It can be said of Antiochus III, hard pressed as he was by Rome after his defeat in 190 B.C.E., that there was good cause for the measures he took, but for Antiochus IV there were no mitigating circumstances. Plundering and pillaging seemed to be part of his natural bent, and by such means he was able to be generous to those whose support he desired. This is the import of v. 24.

War with Egypt irrupted mainly because of foolish advice given Ptolemy VI by two counsellors whose ambitions outstripped their abilities. It was soon discovered that Ptolemy's forces were no match for those of Antiochus, and the young king himself was taken captive (vv. 25-26). When the two court counsellors transferred their allegiance to the king's brother, and had him proclaimed monarch as Ptolemy VII Euergetes, Egypt found itself with a pair of kings. Cleopatra, the queen mother, and the one who had thwarted her father Antiochus III's plans (v. 17), had died shortly before this and, with her death, poor counsel and downright duplicity became the marks of Egyptian foreign policy. This played into the hands of the astute Antiochus, who was quick to take every advantage. The two kings of v. 27 are Ptolemy VI and Antiochus IV — the latter frequently 'bent on mischief', the former a novice by comparison. Antiochus's pretence of support for Ptolemy VI might well have netted him some gain had not internal Seleucid matters called for his return. It was not yet 'the end' for Egypt, nor for the triumph of God's plan for the nations (v. 27), an event always in the forefront of the author's mind (8:17, 26; 10:14; 11:27, 35). As there is one beginning from which all things spring, so there is one end to which all things move. That is the key to apocalyptic eschatology.

The historical veracity of 2 Maccabees may be open to question, but from time to time its record of events, when these can be otherwise substantiated, makes interesting reading, not least for its colourful attention to detail. In 2 Macc. 5:5-20 there is a vivid account of Antiochus's hurried departure from Egypt and his sacking of Jerusalem, and it is this that provides the background to v. 28. What had alarmed the king, as it turned out, was not a general Judean uprising, but an attempt by the banished Jason (see under v. 22) to regain control, an action prompted by a rumour that Antiochus had died. Both Jason and Jerusalem were to find out that such, indeed, was not the case. It was early in 169 B.C.E. when Antiochus, 'raging inwardly' (2 Macc. 5:11), entered the Holy City. A great massacre ensued. The figure of eighty thousand in 2 Maccabees is doubtless an exaggeration, but some strong tradition about a pitiless slaughter must be behind it. The account goes on to describe how Antiochus, guided by the reinstated puppet Menelaus, 'dared to enter the most holy temple in all the world' (2 Macc. 5:15), how he took what he could lay his hands on, and how he departed, leaving in his wake a stricken and grieving city (see also 1 Macc. 1:20-28). With hindsight it is possible to declare that there could never again be peace between Jerusalem and Antioch. Even at this stage in his reign Antiochus was being forced by his own policies, domestic and foreign, to adopt tactics that would increase in their ruthlessness.

There were enemies within, but even more significantly, Antiochus had failed to take account of the threat of Rome, which had already acted to curb his Egyptian ambitions, and was shortly to do so again. Ambitious and arrogant monarchs, however, are not given to reading the signs of the times. In 168 B.C.E., in response to the reconciliation effected between the two royal brothers in Egypt, and fearful of the consequence of this, Antiochus again invaded that land. But as the author of Daniel, casting it in the form of a prophecy, comments, 'it shall not be this time as it was before' (v. 29). He penetrated Egypt as far as the environs of Alexandria, but was there confronted by the Roman consul, Gaius Popillius Laenas. The 'ships of Kittim' (v. 30a) had arrived. But more than that; they controlled the seas, and Antiochus was placed at a decided disadvantage. Popillius was quick to press the point and, in one of the most amusingly bizarre episodes of ancient times, extracted from Antiochus the promise that he would withdraw his forces and return northwards. What happened was that the Seleucid monarch was literally and physically encircled. A circle was drawn around him, and a response demanded, before he would be permitted to step beyond its circumference. Thus, beaten and humiliated, enraged and vengeful, he retreated north (v. 30). Again it was Jerusalem that was to feel the full measure of that rage, and to be the hapless victim of his vengeance. He poured out his full fury 'against the holy covenant' (v. 30b); the apostates alone were safe. The excuse for this further attack came from the failure of his appointee, 'Philip, by birth a Phrygian' (2 Macc. 5:22), to keep order within the city. Antiochus himself may have entered Jerusalem on this occasion, but the account in 2 Maccabees makes mention only of the measures taken by Apollonius, in agreement with v. 31a. The Seleucid commander entered Jerusalem speaking 'peaceable words' (1 Macc. 1:30), but then set about putting the city to the sword (1 Macc. 1:29-40; 2 Macc. 5:24-26).

The first attack occurred on the sabbath; the odds were all in favour of the enemy. As little remained in the temple to loot, Antiochus having already helped himself, Apollonius proceeded to profane the sanctuary itself. Harsh measures were introduced to erase the faith of Judaism. The sacrificial system was completely dismantled; the burnt offerings and other sacrifices were proscribed; so, too, was circumcision; and the keeping of the Torah became a felony. In other words, the faith of the Hebrew people came under the most concerted and severe attack of its long history.

The crowning insult to a people who throughout the centuries had protected their monotheistic belief and practice from the inroads of alien cults was the setting up of 'the abomination that makes desolate' ('the abomination of desolation') (v. 31), and the introduction into the sacred temple of the worship of Zeus Olympius (2 Macc. 6:1-2). The first sacrifice to this imposed god was offered on 15 Kislev (7 Dec.) 167 B.C.E. Three full years were to pass before this symbol of religious and political persecution was removed. In the course of those three years the divisions within the people became more obvious and more rigid. On the one hand were those who accepted the proscriptions and the innovations as not much more than a further necessary compromise (v. 32a). In some sense it was for them the inevitable concomitant of the gymnasium (the typically Hellenistic centre of higher education; see 1 Macc. 1:14f. and 2 Macc. 4:9-14) and the unavoidable consequence of the confluence of Judaism and Hellenism. On the other hand or, rather, on the other side, were those 'who knew their God' and who determined that, come what may, they would 'stand firm and take action' (v. 32b).

Some six centuries earlier the prophet Hosea, in circumstances less desperate but nonetheless demanding, castigated his contemporaries for their apostasy, for serving not the God of their fathers but the *baalim* of the Canaanites. With understandable prophetic hyperbole he declared that there was 'no faithfulness or kindness, and no knowledge of God in the land' (Hos. 4:1). For Hosea, knowledge of God and active obedience to his will were the two sides of the same coin. The author of Daniel, steeped in the spirit as well as the letter of the prophets, was of like mind, but he acknowledged that among his people were those who would succumb neither to the wiles of Antiochus nor to his threats. These were 'the wise' among the people who, though 'for some days' they may 'fall by sword and flame', would succeed in bringing understanding to 'many', and so keep the faith alive (v. 33). This verse contains two terms which require explanation. First, 'the wise' (*hammaskilim*) is an expression to be found in a number of places in Daniel, but the occurrence of the plural noun here (v. 33), as well as in v. 35 and 12:3, 10, suggests that it is not only a technical term, but one commonly known to the readers. For this reason commentators are inclined to see in this a reference to a special group of the faithful which was a forerunner of the *hasidim* of slightly later times. There is also a strong link at this point with the technical language of some of the writings of the Qumran community. In the latter, the Maskil is one who not only imparts enlightenment and understanding, in accordance with biblical usage of the word, but is a particular functionary within the community (G. Vermes, *The Dead Sea Scrolls in English*, 22). The other term, 'the many' (*harabbim*), occurs often without any technical connotation. Here, in v. 33, it may hint at the notion of an identifiable entity, the congregation of the faithful, those who have responded to the teaching and example of 'the wise'. At Qumran the word *harabbim* does have a clear technical sense. It is they who comprise the community itself.

These brief notes do not exhaust the significance of these two terms. In a number of places throughout the book of Daniel the author's keen interest in prophetic statements is clearly in evidence, e.g., at 9:2 and 24. These are made to serve his particular purpose, and have received attention because they are capable of further interpretation. In other words, in the course of his work, the author presents his readers with a *pesher* on certain biblical texts. In an article entitled 'The Oldest Interpretation of the Suffering Servant' (*VT* 3 [1953]: 400-404), H. L. Ginsberg argued cogently for the recognition of Dan. 12:3 as the author's accepted fulfilment of the so-called Fourth Servant Song. There is much about the language and thought of v. 33 that could extend such a recognition to this verse, too. Indeed, so closely are 11:33 and 12:3 related that what may be said of the one must be said of the other. The application of Isa. 52:13 – 53:12 to this text does not mean that it may not be applied to another.

The observation, as early as Porphyry (a philosopher opposed to both Judaism and Christianity who died in 304 C.E.), that the 'little help' of v. 34a is a reference to the forces of the Maccabees has much to commend it. The alternative interpretation would be to see it as referring to the limited effectiveness of the stand taken by the faithful, but that would be contrary to the tenor of the book as a whole. What ineffectiveness there was could be traced to the insincerity of those who found it opportune, in response to the punitive measures of the Maccabees, to join themselves to the faithful (v. 34b). The Jewish patriots, first under Mattathias and then under Judas, made little distinction between the troops of Antiochus and the apostates among their own nationals. Though it may have been tempting to see in the Hasmoneans the saviours of Israel, the author inclined away from that course. For him the true representatives of the faith were those who eschewed the use of arms, and who suffered even to the point of martyrdom. He believed that it was they who in the end would be vindicated (v. 35). In this his view differed somewhat from that of 1 Enoch 90:9-12.

The subject of vv. 36-39 continues to be Antiochus IV Ephiphanes. Over the years, however, various other interpretations have been advanced. Among medieval Jewish commentators some understood these verses as a reference to the Fourth Kingdom, and this they identified as the Roman empire. Indeed, Rashi makes this identification from v. 21 onwards. On this reckoning, v. 31 has to do, not with the building of the altar to Zeus in 176 B.C.E., but with the desolation and destruction of the temple by the Roman general Titus in 70 C.E., and v. 34 with the abortive Bar Kokhba revolt of 132-135 C.E. On the basis of this chronology the subject of vv. 36ff. is the Roman emperor Constantine I (280-337 C.E.). Ibn Ezra is often at variance with Rashi so far as the identification of the kingdoms and personages of the book of Daniel is concerned, but on vv. 36-39 the two are in general agreement. This is, by and large, the traditional, though not necessarily the modern, Jewish view.

Early Christian commentators, and a few in more recent times, understood this section, and others, in the book of Daniel to be a presaging of the antichrist. Though this has been a tenacious interpretation over the centuries, it now has minimal appeal beyond the circle of some sects, and there would be almost general scholarly agreement with di Lella that such a view is 'exegetically witless and religiously worthless' (*Daniel*, 303).

What we are given in vv. 36-39 is a thumbnail sketch of Antiochus. He is presented as an arrogant and ruthless tyrant, a man who, in his mad quest for power, was heedless even of his own traditions, bent only on the pursuit of self-glorification. Just three years after his accession he took on himself the title Epiphanes, 'god manifest'.

It is the unparalleled effrontery of Antiochus in his blasphemous attack on 'the God of gods', and his self-elevation, even above those gods he himself recognised, that appalled the writer. But nothing could restrain him. The author is forced to admit that he did as he pleased, and would continue to do so until the appointed time, 'for what is determined shall be done' (v. 36). The one God who might have thwarted him chooses not to do so, for the time being at least. The other gods are powerless to intervene, not even to save themselves from oblivion. Like petty vassals they have been brushed aside, even Adonis-Tammuz, 'the one beloved by women' (v. 37), whose attractions had enticed Jewish women in the time of Ezekiel (Ezek. 8:14).

There was a god, however, that did receive the gifts and the obeisance of Antiochus, 'the god of fortresses' (v. 38). It should be noted that both vv. 38 and 39 have translation difficulties. On the assumption that the text was originally in Aramaic, and that the translator misread at certain points, Hartman (*Daniel*, 272 and 302) has provided a more intelligible reading. His recourse to transposition of words in v. 38, however, somewhat weakens his case so far as that verse is concerned. If the RSV reading is correct, it is most likely the god Zeus that is referred to in v. 38a.

The 'strongest fortresses' of v. 39a would be, not simply the Akra as Lacocque suggests (*Daniel*, 232), but the walled city of Jerusalem as well as provincial citadels. A better translation of the early part of v. 39, which does not necessitate any consonantal alteration to the MT and which is suggested by many commentators, is: 'He shall man the strongest fortresses with people [troops] of a foreign god . . .'. This is in keeping with Antiochus's policy.

The Seleucid monarch's beneficence towards those who supported him is the subject of v. 39b. The overall picture that we are given of him is of one who distributed largesse to his friends with the same liberality that he dispensed death to his enemies.

40-45 Up to this point in ch. 11 we have been dealing with the author's presentation, sometimes very succinct, of historical events that bore on the life of the Jewish people from the end of the Babylonian Exile (539 B.C.E.) to the outbreak of the Antiochian persecution. It has been couched in the form of prediction, but it is transparently 'prophecy after the event'. The remaining verses of ch. 11 are of a different order. They are not reflection on the past, but an attempt to presage those events that immediately preceded the death of Antiochus, as well as an account of the death itself.

It is the nature of biblical prophecy that its strength lies, not in the accurate prediction of details, but in the confident intoning of a divine message. The classical prophets were not petty soothsayers; they were proclaimers of the Word of God. Their God-given intelligence and acuity were not somehow suspended in order that they might become the inspired automatons of that same God. A reading of the prophets soon discloses that the relationship between divine inspiration and human perception is far more sophisticated, and far more complex, than that. The effectiveness of the preaching of Amos is not lessened if it is admitted that his inspired words against the surrounding nations (Amos 1:1 – 2:5) are not independent of his keen knowledge of regional and past current affairs. Nor should we seek to dissociate the perspicacity of Isaiah from his divinely ordered confrontation with King Ahaz in ch. 7. Moreover, and this probably bears more closely on the nature of the material of Dan. 11:40-45, the prophet Jeremiah delivered his message of warning to Judah as one very much conversant with the politics of the nations of the ancient Near East, convinced of an impending threat that would bring disaster on a recalcitrant people, and prepared to postulate that the gravest threat would emanate from 'the foe from the north' (Jer. 1:14-15). That the calamity that ineluctably befell Judah and Jerusalem came at the hands of easterners, the Babylonians, and not from the northerners, the Scythians perhaps, was no comfort to those who refused to heed his word. As ever, the detail was secondary to the message.

For a century or more, the pattern of events in the region that enveloped Syria, Palestine, and Egypt was such that the author of Daniel could view the future as having an element of predictability. Short of a surprising diminishing of the ambition of Antiochus, it could be projected that the relationships between the two great feuding nations would not take any unexpected forms. The 'king of the north' and 'the king of the south' were not likely to tread anything but a well-worn political path. Far more predictable, however, was that the scourge of the faithful, the hated, tyrannical Antiochus IV, would, like his predecessors, fall. That the author of Daniel is far more than just an astute political observer is borne out, not by the accuracy or otherwise of the details such as exact time and locale, but by the confident expectation that the remaining days of the Seleucid monarch were truly numbered.

At v. 40 we approach what was for the author the great climax, the beginning of 'the end'. There is no extant record of further warfare between the Ptolemies and the Seleucids at this time. The pattern already established, however, would readily suggest that such might very well be the case, with victory going to 'the king of the north', and serious losses being sustained, as ever, by those who dwell in Palestine. At the time when this was written the Maccabean revolt was well under way, first under the leadership of Mattathias, and then, shortly before his death, under his son Judas (1 Macc. 2:1 – 5:68). That there is no specific mention of the many engagements between the Syrian and Jewish forces is not surprising, for the author saw the will of God fulfilled, not in armed insurgency, but in faithful obedience to Torah and, if need be, in martyrdom. Failure to mention the last campaign of Antiochus, against the Parthians, would also suggest that a probable date of writing is later 165 B.C.E.

In his southward march (vv. 41-43) Antiochus is shown to spare 'Edom and Moab and the main part of the Ammonites' (v. 41b). It makes little sense to regard these words as a later insertion; their interpretation is made no more clear thereby. In all likelihood, what is meant is that these age-old enemies of Israel threw in their lot with Antiochus. The stance, too, of the nation's inveterate foes is predictable.

In this presaged campaign Antiochus is much more successful than in the two which did in fact take place. With no Roman presence to thwart his plans, he adds to his spoils the treasures of Egypt and the farthest reaches of the southern empire. The lands of 'the Libyans and the Ethiopians' are overrun by his troops (v. 43). But, as has happened before, news of unrest in 'the east and the north' alarms him (v. 44). It may be that Maccabean victories prompted such a speculation, but in the course of events, as history has recorded them, it was the Parthians who had begun to undermine an already unstable Seleucid hegemony.

Once more it is the faithful who will bear the brunt of Antiochus's fury (v. 44). But the divine plan, the firm writing (10:21), must run its measured course. Surrounded still by the symbols of victory, the king of the north 'shall come to his end, with none to help him' (v. 45). The language of these verses is very much coloured by that of Ezekiel 38 and 39. An account of the last days of Antiochus is to be found in 1 Macc. 6:1-17, with some colourful additions in 2 Macc. 9:1-29. According to these he died somewhere in Persia, probably near Isfahan; whereas the Daniel prediction, influenced very much by Ezekiel, had him meet his end within that corridor of land 'between the sea and the glorious holy mountain' (12:45).

The artificial chapter division at this point should not be allowed to obscure the very real nexus between 11:45 and 12:1.

CHAPTER 12

THE END AND THE RESURRECTION
Daniel 12:1-13

1-3 The historical connection between 12:1 and the concluding verses of ch. 11 must not be lost sight of. The immediate context of vv. 1-3 is clear beyond question and is integral to a proper understanding of their significance. Antiochus has served his purpose and is about to share the fate of all those monarchs, great and small, who have preceded him. This, of course, is in keeping with the message of chs. 2, 7, and 8. The great turmoil, now about to strike the nation, is made to coincide with the last days of the most detested of all Seleucid rulers. For him 'the end' has come. But there is more in v. 1 than that. Its strongly eschatological character is hinted at in the use of the opening words 'at that time', and their occurrence twice more in the same verse. Three times in all the reader is made to hear the sound of a phrase that resounded ominously in the ears of those who lived in desperate days. The very real possibility that these words have a deliberately evocative purpose must not be discounted. For they immediately call to mind the language of Joel 3:1, 18 (RSV); Isa. 26:1; 27:1, 2, 12, 13, as well as the frequently occurring 'on that day' in Zechariah 12 – 14.

In a thought-provoking essay, J. Blenkinsopp recalls the apocalyptic additions that have been made to some prophetic books. He proffers the suggestion that these have come from circles earlier than the time of Daniel, say, the 3rd cent. B.C.E. From these circles to the book of Daniel, he claims, there is an arguable line of descent ('Interpretation and the Tendency to Sectarianism: An Aspect of Second Temple History', in *Jewish and Christian Self-Definition*, 2:21). Blenkinsopp is wisely cautious, and acutely aware of the difficulties in any attempt to fill in the gaps that unfortunately exist in our understanding of the Judaism of this period, yet his thesis has much to commend it. The book of Daniel did not rise out of a vacuum. Though the identification of its theological precursors may be an intimidating exercise, it is nevertheless one that should be attempted. If the thesis alluded to is correct, this would allow us to see the opening verses of ch. 12 as heralding something far more significant than the mere final eclipse of Antiochus IV. To say this, however, is not to lose sight of the immediate and, partly at least, circumscribing context of this brief apocalypse.

In 12:1, at last the role of Michael receives fuller attention than elsewhere in the book. He is no longer simply 'one of the chief princes' (10:13), nor even 'your prince' (10:21), but 'the great prince who has charge of your people'. The RSV rendering, while not entirely unsatisfactory, could be strengthened somewhat. Hartman's translation, 'the great prince, the protector of your people', though not exhausting the possibilities of the underlying Hebrew, is to be preferred. With the use of the Hebrew *sar* (prince) the military nature of Michael's role is shown to be paramount. He is the one who contends for his people Israel (see 10:13). The word translated 'protector', however, may also have a juridical connotation, and this has been cogently argued by G. W. E. Nickelsburg (*Resurrection, Immortality, and Eternal Life in Intertestamental Judaism*, 11-14). The setting of certain late prophetic collections such as Isaiah 24 – 27 and Zechariah 12 – 14, which undoubtedly prepare the way for the book of Daniel, is one of judgment on the nations that surrounded Israel, but a necessary prerequisite of that is an already executed judgment and refining of Israel itself. These two aspects have a place in 12:1-2. The time being ushered in is a 'time of trouble' (Jer. 30:7), a time of great distress for the nation, for which the words of Zech. 14:2 provide a striking analogue:

> For I will gather all the nations against Jerusalem to battle, and the city shall be taken and the houses plundered and the women ravished; half of the city shall go into exile, but the rest of the people shall not be cut off from the city.

The final destruction is not yet to be. Despite the great tribulation, some of the populace will escape or, with the RSV, 'be delivered'. These are those whose names are 'written in the book'.

For the hinterland of such a concept it is not necessary to go back as far in time as the Babylonian 'tables of fate'. There is material much nearer to hand than that. Malachi 3:16 refers to 'a book of remembrance' in which were written the names of those 'who feared the LORD and thought on his name'. The notion of a book or register being kept by God is fairly common, and appears in such texts as Exod. 32:32; Pss. 69:28; 139:16; Isa. 4:3; and Ezek. 13:9. It is also to be found in extracanonical Jewish literature, e.g., 1 Enoch 108:3, and in the Qumran document The Words of the Heavenly Lights. In the NT it occurs in Phil. 4:3 and quite often, as would be expected, in the Apocalypse (Rev. 3:5; 13:8; 17:8; 20:12, 15), where it is referred to as 'the book of life'.

Whether or not 12:2 is, as is often claimed, the first clear reference to resurrection in the Hebrew Scriptures depends on the view taken of Isa. 26:19. The assertion that the latter text explicitly speaks of an individual resurrection is made with force by some scholars but rejected with equal vigour by others. These see in it, not a promise of the resurrection of the person, but a prediction of the restoration or revivification of the nation in parallel with Ezek. 37:11-14. Whatever the outcome of that debate, it is more than likely that the author of Daniel had the Isaianic text in mind. His keen knowledge of the prophets, already amply demonstrated, would not have permitted him to overlook so seminal a statement. The expressions 'those who sleep in the dust of the earth shall awake' (v. 2a) and 'O dwellers in the dust, awake . . .' (Isa. 26:19) are sufficiently alike to put the issue beyond doubt. This euphemistic circumlocution for death also appears in Jeremiah and Job (Jer. 51:39, 57; Job 14:12; cf. Job 3:13), and 'the dust', as a reference to either the grave itself or to Sheol, is to be found in Isa. 26:19; Job 7:2; 17:16; and Eccl. 3:20.

Throughout the Hebrew Scriptures Sheol is regarded as a place of shadowy existence and certainly not a place of punishment. It is that cavernous region below the earth where the life-force is no longer present and where personality no longer counts. In Sheol everything sheds its vitality. This is nowhere better summarised than in the words of Qohelet, 'better a live dog than a dead lion' (Eccl. 9:4). For the same author, man's ultimate destination is no better than that of the animals (Eccl. 3:19). A thoughtfully despondent note is to be found in certain psalms where it is lamented that Sheol is even beyond God's reach (Pss. 6:5; 88:4-12). The psalmist bemoans the fact that the God whom he has served for a lifetime will no longer be present with him in death. To add to the complexity of the matter, so far as early Hebrew religion was concerned, for the prophet Amos Sheol came within the bounds of God's domain:

> 'Though they dig into Sheol,
>   from there shall my hand take them;
> though they climb up to heaven,
>   from there I will bring them down'. (Amos 9:2)

The universalism of the eighth-century prophet would not allow the grave a last claim, though he leaves no conspicuous trace of any belief in life after death.

In any attempt to trace within ancient Hebrew religion the development of a belief in the afterlife, or the factors that were influential in that development, certain points require attention. Very briefly stated these are:

(i) The God of the ancient Hebrew is firmly embedded in the faith as a Creator God. Clearly this is so in the exilic and postexilic periods. Consequently, the need arose for seeing God as having no limits placed on him. Death, for a long time accepted as the natural lot of man, came to be reckoned as an interloper in a world where creation and life were synonymous. This is best summarised in a later (1st cent. B.C.E.) text: '. . . God did not make death, and he does not delight in the death of the living' (Wis. 1:13).

(ii) God is omnipotent and his rule is universal. This is closely related to (i) and is best exemplified by reference to Amos 9:2.

(iii) The bond between the faithful believer and the God of his devotion was such that the lament at the thought of the permanent loss of fellowship gave way to the belief that death must no longer be seen as a barrier between the two.

(iv) The God of the Torah and of the prophets is a God of justice. The time would arrive when a facile explanation of the injustices dealt out to the faithful would no longer be acceptable. Jeremiah struggled with the problem of theodicy (Jer. 12:1), as did his contemporary Habakkuk (Hab. 1:13), and later, perhaps also Job.

To what extent some or all of these factors influenced the author of the book of Daniel is impossible to determine. Certainly, the question of theodicy must have been present. Moreover, it is not easy to identify or assess possible extra-Hebraic influences such as those of Iranian religion or Greek thought.

The 'many' of v. 2 places a strict limitation on the use to which this verse may be put. The author's concern is not with all ages of mankind, but with two particular groupings within his own people. The events of the past decade or so had given rise to a cleavage within the Jewish people. On the one side were the faithful (1 Macc. 1:60-63), and on the other the apostates (1 Macc. 1:52). The criterion by which one was separated from the other was simple and straightforward. The author's contemporaries had a choice, obedience to the Torah or obedience to the decree of Antiochus IV (1 Macc. 1:41ff.). Some would awake to 'everlasting life' and others to 'shame and everlasting contempt'. When v. 2 is examined closely, it can be seen that it leaves many questions unanswered. It speaks only of those who have died, presumably as a result of the 'time of trouble' (v. 1). Nothing is said of the fate of the faithful of earlier times, nor is it possible to see in the brief mention of the lot of the apostates any clear reference to punishment. The extent of the resurrection is unclear; so, too, is its nature. Though 12:2 may point towards something beyond its immediate context, it is not possible, from the brevity of the verse itself, to spell out its contours. For all its importance it is only a step along the way. The development in thought about life beyond the grave was taken up in later Jewish writings, e.g., 1 Enoch 51:1-5, 2 Macc. 7:7-23, and the Wisdom of Solomon where the idea of retribution is to the fore (Wis. 2–4; 6:1-11). The extension of the belief in resurrection and retribution, and the concomitant emphasis on man's immortality, are to be found in the teaching of the Pharisees. These were taken up by later (post-70 C.E.) Judaism where they received the stamp of orthodoxy. Here, as elsewhere in matters of faith, the Pharisees, the more progressive element within Judaism, differed with the Sadducees. New Testament doctrine has much in common with that of Pharisaic Judaism, though it has its own contribution to make to the subject. So, too, has the Qumran literature, yet unexpectedly among the Dead Sea sectaries the notion of resurrection as such appears to have receded into the background.

Verse 3 has to do with a special category within the faithful, the *maskilim* (11:33, 35; 12:10). It is these who 'shall shine like the brightness of the firmament'. This type of language has prompted some scholars to see here some influence of astral religion, either Iranian or Greco-Roman. Needless to say, opinions differ sharply. A more important exegetical point is the evident relationship between v. 3b and the figure of the servant in the fourth of the so-called Servant Songs (see under 11:33 above). The parallelism of v. 3 suggests that not two groups but one is spoken of. They are 'the wise' who 'bring many to righteousness', i.e., not only are they themselves faithful upholders of Torah, but they lead others in the way. Isaiah 53:11 says of the servant: 'By his knowledge shall the righteous one, my servant, make many to be accounted righteous'. The links between the servant of Isa. 52:13 – 53:12, the servants of Trito-Isaiah, and the *maskilim* of Dan. 12:3 are brought out clearly in the study by Nickelsburg already referred to (*Resurrection*, 25). The identification at this point does not preclude any later attempted identification, but it itself must be taken with the utmost seriousness.

For the first time in the Hebrew Scriptures there is clear evidence of the emergence of a group which saw itself as the bearers of the nation's traditional role, the Israel of God. It would be to go beyond the available evidence to suggest that this necessarily heralded the rise of Jewish sects, but it is in this period, one of great turmoil, of claim and counterclaim, that one can see the circumstances that might quite naturally lead to the fracturing of the one people of God.

4 Daniel has previously been commanded (8:26b) to 'seal up the vision'. Now, at the conclusion of the last and longest vision, he is again directed to 'shut up the words, and seal the book, until the time of the end'. The seal will be broken and the truth unleashed only when the appointed time dawns, and this was known only to those who had eyes to see and ears to hear.

The second part of v. 4 is not without textual problems. There are two possible renderings. The first adheres to the MT and the translation of the RSV. This preserves a possible link with Amos

8:12, which foresees a time when men 'shall run to and fro, to seek the word of the Lord' but fail to find it. The second requires the slightest of slight emendations to the consonantal text, and would give a reading: 'Many shall run to and fro, and calamities will multiply'. There is some support for the latter in the LXX.

5-13 These verses constitute an epilogue or conclusion to the entire book. The vision proper reached its climax at v. 3, with the following verse as the final instruction. There are still some unanswered questions, however, and it is these that now receive belated attention. The rather unnatural relationship of these verses to what precedes them should warn us against any attempt at identification of 'the man clothed in linen' beyond that already made in ch. 10. As for the 'two others', these would appear to be the required witnesses to the oath (v. 7), in accordance with Deut. 19:15. The setting is necessarily the same as that of the long vision, by the banks of the river Tigris (10:4).

The most pressing of all the apocalyptist's questions is reiterated: 'How long?' (v. 6). The RSV translation, 'wonders', gives the opposite effect to that intended. What is being referred to is the extraordinary events that accompanied the reign of Antiochus. A related Hebrew word is used in 8:24, '. . . and he shall cause fearful destruction . . .' .

The appearance of the 'two others' (v. 5) has to do with the swearing of the oath in v. 7. It is a legal requirement, stated quite explicitly in Deut. 19:15, that no charge can be sustained unless there are two or three corroborating witnesses. In this context, it is the crime of Antiochus against God's people that necessitates such a precaution. The elaborate oath-swearing ceremony depicted in v. 7, with not merely one arm raised but the two, is entirely for Daniel's benefit. Daniel's hesitancy has to be circumvented. The oath is taken in the name of 'him who lives for ever', recalling the divine epithet of 4:34. In pronouncing that the span of time is to be 'for a time, two times, and half a time', a ready link is made with both 7:25 and 9:27. In this reassuring and painstakingly confirmatory word to Daniel nothing is added; it is a reiteration of what he has already been told. But neither has anything been subtracted. If Daniel had good reason to see his faith confirmed by this exercise, he had equally good reason to see his fears confirmed as well. The time of turmoil, the time of agony for his people, is not to be curtailed. God's plan must run its course, and it is this, no doubt, that prompts his question in v. 8. That there should be a period of waiting before 'the end' is what Daniel has difficulty in understanding. The victims have a right to question the inexorability of suffering, much more so when it seems to have on it the imprimatur of the deity. But Daniel's expression of concern is cut short with the words, 'Go your way. . .'. His half-hearted attempt to stall the inevitable is brushed aside, perhaps not peremptorily, but certainly effectively. What is written must stand. The words are sealed 'until the time of the end' (v. 9), and Daniel must accept that that is so.

Nor is there much comfort for Daniel in v. 10. Again the two strict categories emerge, the obedient and the disobedient, the faithful and the apostate, those who through their suffering will be refined, and those who through their blindness will be confirmed in their own wickedness. It is with the statements of vv. 9 and 10 that apocalyptic presents its most difficult face. There is great appeal in the unequivocal assertion that the evil forces of this world will be overcome at some given point in history. It may be comforting, especially in times of crisis and persecution, to reflect on the ultimate victory of goodness and righteousness, and the total eclipse of injustice. But this theological worldview is not without its problems, not the least of which is the rigid determinism which it entails. In the 'go your way', twice addressed to Daniel (vv. 9 and 13), there is a repudiation of all earthly effort to usher in the kingdom of God except by the most passive means. Apocalyptic eschatology allows no compromise where compromise might be thought to be the most acceptable solution. Intelligent reading of the book of Daniel demands that all romantic notions of a forthcoming era of bliss be sublimated, and that the stark theological issues be faced honestly and frankly. Different readers may come to different conclusions, but the questions themselves dare not be overlooked.

In 8:14 we were informed that the period during which the 'continual burnt offering' would be proscribed would be 'two thousand and three hundred evenings and mornings', i.e., 1150 days. This matter is complicated by the statement in 12:11 that the duration will be 1290 days and by the appearance in v. 12 of the figure, 1335 days. Quite often the difficulty is met by taking

1290 as the first corrected figure and 1335 as the second. That is to say, they are successive glosses made in order to give the original prediction some shade of historical verisimilitude. That both vv. 11 and 12 should be permitted to remain in the text is sufficient commentary on this rather unadroit explanation. A more acceptable solution may be that the figure in v. 11 is in fact a correction of that in 8:14, for the subject matter of the verses seems to be the same. The 1335 days of v. 12, however, does not specifically refer to the proscription of the 'continual burnt offering' and in all likelihood has in mind an event to take place after the cleansing of the temple. The focal point of the last vision is 'the end', but it is clear that this is to coincide with the demise of Antiochus Epiphanes (11:45 – 12:3). 'Blessed is he who waits and comes to the thousand three hundred and thirty-five days' points forward to that day. It is no more accurate than the 1150 or the 1290; like them it is a predicted figure. But it is the prediction of a different event, the cataclysmic appearance of Michael on behalf of his people.

The concluding verse of the book is a word of assurance to Daniel himself. Long before the predicted events take place he will go to his 'rest'. The pessimism of Qohelet offers this solace at least, 'there is no work . . . in Sheol' (Eccl. 9:10). But Sheol will not hold the faithful Daniel. He is heir to the promise of resurrection, and 'at the end of the days' will take his stand in his 'allotted place' (v. 13). This is a fitting reward for a man who, since the early days of the Exile, has stood firm against temptation and threat.

The book of Daniel has from time to time exerted considerable influence on Christian thought. This influence extends as far back as some of the NT writers, if not to Jesus himself. A thorough investigation of this would amount to a study in itself. Our immediate purpose is met if we single out two areas for relatively brief mention.

The first Gospel to be written, Mark, contains a long discourse in its thirteenth chapter, attributed by the writer to Jesus. This chapter contains some thirty instances of knowledge or use of the text of Daniel. In an exhaustive treatment of the provenance of Mark 13, L. Hartman concluded that 'perhaps the apocalyptic ideas in Daniel played a more important part in Jesus' thinking than modern, nonapocalyptic, sober-minded western scholars may imagine at first glance' (*Prophecy Interpreted,* 250). Not all scholars have been unaware of this possible influence on Jesus, but at times the suggestion that it may have been formative has been stoutly resisted. Just as stoutly resisted has been the claim that early Christian theological formulation is dependent in no small way on apocalyptic thought. If this contention is presented in clear-cut black-and-white terms, or if it is put forward as a peculiarly Christian in contradistinction to a Jewish world view, it loses some of its credibility. But that there was a strong element of apocalyptic in early Christian theology is beyond question.

The second area of influence, which may not necessarily be confidently cited in any attempt to establish Jesus' own position but which assists the above argument, is associated with the book of Revelation. The links between this book and certain OT prophetic works such as Ezekiel and Second Isaiah are clear beyond doubt. But it is not possible to read Revelation without becoming aware of its many points of contact with the book of Daniel. One of the issues that is difficult to resolve is whether the author of Revelation was guided by what the writer of Daniel had in mind, or whether he found in the work of the latter simply a repository of language and imagery which fostered his own purpose. Whatever the answer might be, it is again clear that the NT writer is presenting a world view that is closer to apocalyptic than to any other of the time.

Surprisingly, references to the figure of Daniel as such are not to be found in the NT. One would think that somewhere there might have been some allusion to Daniel the man of prayer, or Daniel the obedient servant of God. Christian tradition since the time of the NT, however, has made ample use of Daniel the man as well as the book that bears his name. There is a long history of this use in art, literature, and music.

Given the dramatic visual quality of the Daniel stories, it is little wonder that these had an attraction for such artists as Rubens (*Daniel and the Lions* [1618]), Rembrandt (*Belshazzar's Feast* [1634] and *Vision of Daniel* [ca. 1652]), and Delacroix (*Daniel and the Lions*). Daniel himself is the subject of a Bernini sculpture (1656) now in the Chigi Chapel in the Church of Santa Maria de Popolo in Rome.

From the rather prosaic seventh-century Anglo-Saxon paraphrase to the imaginative black American sermons of Vachel

Lindsay's *Daniel Jazz* (1920), the book has greatly enriched the literature of the English-speaking world.

In the field of music there is the Handel oratorio, *Belshazzar* (1745), and, in more recent times, Benjamin Britten's *The Burning Fiery Furnace* (1966). The black American spiritual *Shadrach, Meshach, and Abednego*, written by Robert McGinney and popularised by the celebrated Louis Armstrong, is further testimony to the influence exerted by these brief but profound presentations of suffering and faith.

It is interesting that there is to be detected in the above more of an interest in, and affinity with, the stories of Daniel than with the visions. In this, our art, literature, and music may simply be reflecting the difficulty that the modern mind has in coming to grips with apocalyptic, even the rather subdued apocalyptic of Daniel. Yet the themes of this type of literature are not at all foreign to us. Injustice, persecution, temptation to apostatize, despair — they are all present in apocalyptic, and certainly in the book of Daniel. The question to which apocalyptic addresses itself is: How best may these be met? Will they be overcome gradually, by the slow attrition of evil and the measured, but inevitable, assertion of good? Or is this process no more than the wishful thinking of naive optimists?

Where there have been exceptions to the modern neglect or even spurning of apocalyptic, these exceptions have emerged during times of helplessness and desperation, when political solutions have proved to be vapid, and social upheaval imminent. In other words, we are more likely to turn to an apocalyptic expression of our fears and our hopes when a situation similar to that which gave it birth appears in our own midst. It is then that some minds at least are given over to the conviction that mankind's best efforts have worn thin, and the sole solution to the ills of this world may be some externally directed cataclysmic intervention. The secular apocalyptist will decide on the ordering and outcome of this according to his own insight. The biblical apocalyptist will be convinced that it must have one source and one alone.

It is not possible to read the book of Daniel without being constantly reminded of two things in particular. The first is that the way of obedience and faith may be attended by dire physical suffering and even death. That this is so has been attested by countless Jews and Christians throughout the centuries, not least in recent times. The second and more consoling observation is this. For all the ignominy and harassment to which men and women of faith may be subjected by powers which seem to have won the day, ultimate victory rests not with those who resort to coercion and brute force, but with God. We are reminded that from the most unlikely source may come the confession:

> How great are his signs,
>   how mighty his wonders!
> His kingdom is an everlasting kingdom,
>   and his dominion is from generation to generation. (4:3)

BIBLIOGRAPHY OF WORKS
CITED

Modern Commentaries

Goldwurm, R. H. *Daniel* (Brooklyn: Mesorah, 1979).

Hartman, L. F. and Di Lella, A. A. *The Book of Daniel*. Anchor Bible (Garden City: Doubleday, 1978).

Heaton, E. W. *The Book of Daniel*. Torch Bible Commentary (London: SCM, 1956).

Lacocque, A. *The Book of Daniel*, trans. D. Pellauer (Atlanta: John Knox, 1979).

Montgomery, J. A. *The Book of Daniel*. International Critical Commentary (Edinburgh: T. & T. Clark, 1927).

Porteous, N. W. *Daniel*, 2nd rev. ed. Old Testament Library (London: SCM and Philadelphia: Westminster, 1979).

Other Works

Black, M. *An Aramaic Approach to the Gospels*: with an Appendix on the Son of Man by Geza Vermes, 3rd ed. (Oxford: Oxford University Press, 1967).

Blenkinsopp, J. 'Interpretation and the Tendency to Sectarianism: An Aspect of Second Temple History' in *Jewish and Christian Self-Definition*, Vol. 2: *Aspects of Judaism in the Greco-Roman Period*, ed. E. P. Sanders (Philadelphia: Fortress, 1981), pp. 1-26.

Casey, M. *Son of Man: The Interpretation and Influence of Daniel 7* (London: SPCK, 1979).

Ginsberg, H. L. 'The Oldest Interpretation of the Suffering Servant', *Vetus Testamentum* 3 (1953): 400-404.

Hartman, L. *Prophecy Interpreted: The Formation of Some Jewish*

157

Apocalyptic Texts and of the Eschatological Discourse, Mark 13 (Lund: Gleerup, 1966).

Hengel, M. *Judaism and Hellenism: Studies in Their Encounter in Palestine during the Early Hellenistic Period*, 2 vols., trans. J. Bowden (London: SCM and Philadelphia: Fortress, 1974).

Käsemann, E. *NT Questions of Today*, trans. W. J. Montague (Philadelphia: Fortress, 1979).

Moore, C. A. *Daniel, Esther and Jeremiah: The Additions*. Anchor Bible (Garden City: Doubleday, 1977).

Nickelsburg, G. W. E. *Resurrection, Immortality, and Eternal Life in Intertestamental Judaism* (Cambridge, Mass.: Harvard University Press, 1972).

Pritchard, J. B., ed. *Ancient Near Eastern Texts relating to the Old Testament*, 3rd ed. (Princeton: Princeton University Press, 1969).

Schürer, E. *The History of the Jewish People in the Age of Jesus Christ (175 B.C. – A.D. 135)*, 2 vols., a new English version rev. and ed. by G. Vermes, F. Millar, and M. Black (Edinburgh T. & T. Clark, 1973-1979).

Steiner, G. *In Bluebeard's Castle: Some Notes Towards the Re-definition of Culture* (London: Faber and New Haven: Yale University Press, 1971).

Vermes, G. *The Dead Sea Scrolls in English*, 2nd ed. (Harmondsworth: Penguin, 1975).